Student Housing Handbook.

Rights, Responsibilities and Resilience in Student Accommodation.

Matthew J. Evans

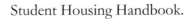

Dedication.

This book is dedicated to all student residential workers who go the extra mile for the students in their care. And to Patrick for putting up with me every day.

Table of contents.

Introduction.

Except for a small children's book written for my daughter, this book marks my first ever literary project and something I have wanted to do for a very long time.

The aim of this book is to give advice to new university and college students on how to prepare for life in higher education and student accommodation, looking at personal safety and their rights and responsibilities. Understanding that for many teens, the first time away from home without that support network can be daunting, especially in the era of social media toxicity and ever-increasing mental health concerns among the age group.

I spent my twenties working as a security officer and in my spare time a self-defence instructor, I have worked with the police and local government organizations and even a human rights lawyer who specialized in self-defence. In my thirties I started work at a university, almost a decade later I work in housing management where I manage student discipline and pastoral care.

I also have experience working as a welfare officer for the FA where I helped to enforce and monitor the respect campaign at grass roots level.

The combination of these experiences gives me a unique outlook on life, and I hope to be able to share some useful tips with you here.

Part One:
The student journey.

The First question to ask yourself before signing up to higher education is why?

What do you hope to achieve? Are you just wanting the experience, the hook ups, and mad parties? If that is your plan it might be cheaper to take a gap year in Ibiza.

When you are picking your degree, it might be worth considering the value of that degree, especially if you are paying an average of £45,000 in three years to study. There are degree calculators available online, but it would be wise to look at the available jobs for people with that degree, what careers they enter into and how much they get paid and so on.

There has been some recent research on the ten degrees that are the worst value for money, by calculating the average salary five years after graduation.

- Photography   £24,785
- Translation   £24,815
- Film   £24,851
- Fine Art   £24,999
- Criminology   £25,069
- Music   £25,348
- English Literature   £26,169
- Events Management   £26,410
- Fashion   £26,435
- Architecture   £26,523

It is worth noting however that there are multiple factors affecting salary, nearly 40% of university degrees do not lead to a salary over £30,000 in the first five years after graduating.

Factors such as not having experience can make it difficult to get your foot on the career ladder.

There are universities that offer more hands-on approach to teaching, which could mitigate the lack of experience by working and studying concurrently. The planned university of Peterborough for example, will be offering a course on events management that will give the students a placement year, I fully expect this to increase the marketability of people with those degrees.

It will serve you well to research your courses and the institutions to find the best fit for you and your chosen career.

I have worked in student accommodation for nearly three years at the time of writing and most students I have spoken to, do not know 'what they want to be' when they leave university. Whilst it is true that having a degree makes you more employable, only around half of UK graduates are working in a field that relates to their degree, in addition around 47% of recent graduates work in a non-graduate field. Did those 47% of graduates waste their money? Or was the experience worth the cost? I will let you decide.

If you are certain you want to attend higher education, I wish you the best on your journey and hope my words here provide some support.

Good luck….

UK higher education costs.

With the UKs Purpose built student accommodation market worth £50 billion and accounting for 31% of global investment there is intense competition between university owned accommodation and the private sector. With increasing student fees and accommodation costs, student expectations are increasing, to get value for their money. This is putting more pressure on universities to keep up with ever rising standards, demands for new technology and modern equipment and buildings.

Rooms in purpose built private sector accommodation can be more expensive but can offer newer, freshly refurbished accommodation with added extras, like gym membership and 24-hour staff cover. Other private sector rooms can be cheaper, but students can be left paying for household bills.

In contrast the unique selling point of university managed accommodation is being on campus, close to events, close to class and close to friends.

Until recently university fees have been capped at £9000 per year for UK students but are now increasing again, currently at £9250. If you come from abroad, you could be paying much more.

Living costs in UK can vary between £800 to £1600 per month for a student depending on location (this includes rents). It is no surprise that London has the highest living costs, rents, and food costs in the

UK, but you do get much higher maintenance loans for living in the capital.

Areas like Milton Keynes, Bath and Reading follow in all three factors as some of the most expensive areas. Followed by the more famous university cities of Cambridge and Oxford.

One reason for this, is the high cost of property in these areas, Cambridge for example ranks 28th of the UK postcode areas for property prices and is 27.5% higher than the average for England and Wales.

In terms of food prices, the most cost-effective cities to live in are Liverpool, Newcastle, Sheffield, Exeter, and Norwich. With Sheffield, Liverpool, and Newcastle being more affordable on rents and general living costs.

The current average weekly rents in the UK are as follows:

- Purpose built student accommodation: £166.
- Private sector ensuite: £155.
- Private sector studio: £228.
- London university accommodation: £212.
- London private sector: £259.

Cheapest universities:

- Ulster university, Derry: £75.
- Bradford, Huddersfield, Bangor £80-85.

Student loans:

As a full-time student, you are entitled to a tuition fee loan, this is paid directly to your institution to pay for your course fees, at this time of writing that is £9250 per year for UK students.

You can claim student fee loans by creating an account with student finance, this can be done anytime up to 9 months after your course has started, however it would be best to have your finances sorted out long before arriving at university.

Specifics on how to set up an account and apply can be found at **https://www.gov.uk/apply-online-for-student-finance**. It is important to note that it can take up to 6 weeks to process your application, so get it resolved as early as possible.

As with all loans, you must pay this loan back, albeit once you graduate and earning over a certain amount, it is important to understand that you start accruing interest from the day you take the loan out.

You become liable for repayments at the start of each term during the year as follows, this is due, even if you withdraw, transfer, or suspend your studies.

- Start of term 1: 25%
- Start of term 2: 50%
- Start of term 3: 100%

For example, if you withdraw from university during term 2 of your second year you would have to repay the first year's tuition fee and 50% of the second years fees.

This would be £13,875 plus interest. Repayments would follow the standard procedures however and would not be something you had to pay right away.

Tuition fees only pay for your courses, in addition to this, you would be entitled to apply for a maintenance loan to help pay for your living costs.

Maintenance loans are paid directly to you at the start of each term, the yearly entitlement would be divided by three terms each year, you would also be obliged to repay these loans even if you withdrew.

For example, if you get £6000 per year, this is £2000 per term, if you withdraw halfway through term 2, you are not entitled to the entire term 2 loan, but you have already been paid, so will have to pay some back at that time. The rest is paid back via the standard means.

The amount of maintenance you are entitled to would depend on your circumstances, if you are currently living at home with your parents, you would receive less than if you live on your own in university accommodation. There are several other factors that determine your entitlement, but assuming you a student in halls the maintenance loan is capped at £9,488 per year, or £12,382 for London.

There are loan calculators online that you can use to determine the exact amount you will receive, this is important for determining you budgets whilst away at university. For most students currently, you could expect £7,831. This will be split equally between three terms and paid at the start of each term.

The combined amount of tuition fees and maintenance fees paid to you (or the institute to pay for course fees) are paid and managed by the student loans company (SLC). The SLC manage your account for the entire life of the loan, adding interest and subtracting payments made.

Payments are made through the PAYE tax system once you start working and earning over £27,295 per year. The average yearly wage in 2021 was £25,971, so you do not start paying your loans back until you earn over the average UK wage.

The repayment amount is calculated at 9% on any earnings over £27,295.

For example, if you earn £33,00 a year you would pay back approximately £42 per month.

As mentioned above, you would start accruing interest on your loans from the moment the first payment is made to you. This is calculated currently at RPI + 3% during the time you study and then vary afterwards depending on your income. If you earn less than the threshold (£27,295) interest drops to base RPI, if you earn over this amount and are making repayments, the interest is calculated at RPI + 3%.

To explain, RPI means retail price index, which is a more precise measurement of inflation that is used to calculate cost of living increases and wage escalation, in 1947 it replaced the cost-of-living index. In essence it tracks the price of items (except food) to determine how much costs increase over time.

Post-graduation you can also make additional payments to the SLC to clear the debt faster, however remaining loans are cancelled 30 years after you are due to start making repayments (graduation).

If you graduate aged 21, your loans will be cancelled when you are 51, regardless of how much you still owe.

Whilst you should be mindful of these repayments, it is not something I would recommend worrying about, even if you withdraw. To put it into context I did not earn the threshold repayment amount until my late thirties, although to be fair I do not yet have my degree.

The biggest worry for most students is the disparity between the maintenance loans and rent payments.

Taking the average rent payment of £166 over a 42-week contract (contracts vary between 40-50 weeks), means a yearly rent total of £6972 and the average maintenance loan of £7,831.

Many of you will have realized that this only leaves £859 for the entire years' worth of food, consumables, clothes, and other necessary items, and that is not even including going out with friends and enjoying life.

On average students spend the following each month:

- Groceries: £101
- Take-aways: £41
- Going out: £47
- Clothes: £34
- Course materials: £17
- Mobile contracts: £15
- Health and wellbeing: £15
- Gifts/charity: £13

This is not an exhaustive list and as you can see the leftover maintenance loan barely scratches a student's expenditure. In fact, most parents help students to the tune of £120 per month on average to assist with these issues.

For most students, this discrepancy means getting a job, which can add more stress and time management worries to an already tense situation.

Worryingly we have seen a recent increase in the number of students turning to sex work to pay the bills, although still a small number, around 10% of students know someone who engages in sex work (prostituting, escorting, lap dancing, stripping, or sending nude pictures). I will discuss this issue in greater detail later.

Be prepared.

So, you have applied to your chosen university, and they sent you an offer. If it is a conditional offer, you still have some work to do, you must get those grades. But whether conditional or unconditional the first thing you should do is book your accommodation, do not wait.

If you do not make the grades on a conditional offer the institute will normally cancel your booking and refund your deposit or advance rent payment (worth checking this prior to booking as every institute has differences), so do not wait around, get booking that room.

Not every institution works the same way, some will allocate you a room, some will let you book your actual chosen room. Either way, view the website for virtual tours, visit the university at open days and view the residential rooms in person, ask as many questions as you need. Are flats mixed gender? where launderettes are (normally parents will ask this), how many people you share a kitchen or bathroom with.

Note that due to data protection, GDPR (General Data Protection Regulation), universities will not be able to give you the names or details of your room mates, however many social media pages will have groups set up for your university/halls of residence and you can quickly find who you are staying with.

Something to remember is that although residential departments are staffed with extremely helpful people (trust me I work with and have met many of them. Worryingly some of them even like me), they deal with thousands of students every year and aside from generic email updates they will not approach you too often.

You need to put yourself forward, ask the questions you have. Its good practice for life to assert yourself and the adage is true "if you don't ask you don't get."

If you want to ask for the floor plans, location of boiler rooms and foot traffic in your area of the building do so. This is your first home away from home and you will be there for the best part of a year, you will want to avoid areas of noise and disturbances.

If you are booking early, there will be some choice, so it pays to ask a few more questions. Do your research on the halls, what have previous students said about it? what do current students say? Are the halls open plan or segregated flats? Are there ensuite or shared bathrooms?

An important note here: Some online reviews will be written by people with an axe to grind, it may be that 99% of people are happy but the 1% speaks louder, that is the double-edged sword of social media and the internet unfortunately. Equally most institutes marketing teams will only want to show the best areas and make everything shiny and perfect to attract you.

Take everything with a pinch of salt and double check.

One of the biggest issues you will face in halls is conflict with flat mates and a part of the reason for that is your expectations, often you do not know what to expect, you may currently have an annoying sibling or have had clashes with parents, but now you are going to live with half a dozen strangers for a year and that is a different challenge entirely.

Use social media to find and connect with your flat mates, find out about each other, are there cultural differences? dietary issues? What are their likes and dislikes? Do they have hairy feet and six toes? learning these things will avoid any potential clashes due to differences in values and allow you all to set expectations before you have even moved in.

This does not guarantee you will avoid conflict, but as Tesco are fond of saying "every little helps."

The best of advice I can give you before moving in, is to read your tenancy agreement and to ask the halls management team if there is a banned item list, although if you read the tenancy agreement you will be able to form your own list based on the points made therein.

You may want to ask if your halls allow mini fridges in rooms? You will find in some cases that cooking items and kettles are banned in bedrooms but check to be sure. You do not want to make the mistake of bringing banned items with you, only to find yourself with a warning for breaching your tenancy agreement.

A generic banned list will probably include, but not be limited to the following items, but every institution will differ to some extent, so it is important to check and not make assumptions:

- Hookahs/Shishas.
- Space heaters (electric convection heaters).

- Candles, incense, oil burners, anything with a naked flame. (Some institutions may allow electric oil burners).
- Flammable gases or liquids, for obvious reasons. Cigarette lighters will be ok to own, but smoking is not permitted in room.
- Pets.
- LED strips, these can damage walls/paintwork and lead to charges.
- Weapons, again obvious. However, there is some grey area in terms of what is considered a weapon.
- Drugs.

Many of these issues will be specified in the tenancy agreement. Drugs are a big issue for student halls. The laws governing student housing management makes it the responsibility of the halls manager if they know drugs are present and they do not act.

In simple terms if they know you have drugs, and this can include prescription drugs (if they are not yours) and do nothing, they can be held legally liable. So, expect them to come down hard on you.

For me, where my job in housing management is concerned, I am far too pretty for prison and will not turn a blind eye to this issue.

In terms of weapons, many things you may think of as weapons have everyday uses, such as kitchen knives. But keeping one under your pillow may raise some questions.

In law, the term 'offensive weapon' is used, and these are categorized into three types:

<u>Type One:</u> Offensive weapons: whose only/main purpose is to cause injury.

<u>Type Two:</u> Items adapted to cause injury: for example, a baseball bat with nails in.

<u>Type Three:</u> Items carried with the intent to cause injury: Hard to define "intent" but if you are walking around the streets with a cricket bat and you are not coming from or going to a cricket game and do not have a cricket ball, the balance of probabilities is that you are not using it for its designed purpose and are intending to use it to cause injury.

There are items which are dangerous that have authentic, lawful purposes such as kitchen knives. However as described above carrying one around in public would likely get you arrested for intending to cause injury.

In fact, UK law stipulates that no knife even when carried publicly for legitimate reasons can have a blade in excess of three inches.

As you ready yourself for student life, be aware of the risks before you arrive. But use this opportunity to ensure you have everything packed, double check and check again.

Depending on the size of your university room and potential storage space, you may not want to pack everything. Check what your university is providing and start with the essentials using the following checklist:

Bedroom.
- Bedding: Duvet, duvet cover, pillows, pillowcases, fitted sheets (know the size of your bed). Additional blankets and cushions.
- Laundry basket.

- Clothes hangers.
- Small drying rack.
- Decorative items such as posters, framed pictures, bedside lamp etc.

Clothes (try not to overpack).
- Everyday comfortable clothes, jeans, shorts, t-shirts, lightweight jumpers, and warm cotton sweatshirts (these are easier to wash and dry than wool items).
- Sports or gym clothes, shorts joggers, vests, and sports bras.
- Cold weather clothes, warm coat (ideally waterproof), hat, gloves, and scarf. You will be at university for nearly a year and will need to pack for all weathers.
- Pyjamas, slippers, and a dressing gown.
- Smart clothes, for nights out and others that are suitable for a part-time job.
- Book bag for day to day use around campus.

Bathroom.
- Wash bag.
- Soap, shower gel and face wash.
- Shampoo and conditioner, hairbrush, comb.
- Bath towels and handtowels.
- Toothpaste and toothbrush.
- Deodorant and/or perfume.
- Razors and shaving cream.
- Toilet roll.
- Tampons, pads.

- Condoms/contraceptives.
- Flip flops or crocs for shared bathrooms.
- First aid items such as painkillers, nail kit, tweezers, and plasters. If you wear glasses record your prescription somewhere safe.

Kitchen items. (Institutes will provide some items such as fridge freezers, ovens, hobs, and microwaves). Try not to buy too much until you arrive or speak to other flatmates before-hand, if you all bring a set of saucepans, most of them will go unused and affect storage space.

- Coffee maker.
- Kettle.
- Toaster.
- Cookware, saucepans, casserole dishes, wok, baking tray etc.
- Crockery, plates, bowls, cups etc.
- Cutlery.
- Glasses, tumblers etc.
- Mixing bowl.
- Wooden spoon.
- Measuring jug.
- Tin opener (crucial).
- Bottle opener or corkscrew.
- Kitchen knives and cutting boards (always use a board to prevent damage, get one for meat one for veg to avoid cross contamination).
- Scissors.
- Tea towels.
- Tupperware and sandwich bags for storage.

- Cling film and tin foil.

Stationary.
You may only want to pack the basics and pick up more after you arrive, although you can save money by preparing long in advance and picking up offers when you see them.

- Pens, pencils, and highlighters.
- Post-it notes.
- A4 paper pads, ideally with sheets that can be torn out.
- Planner or diary.
- Ring binders and plastic wallets.
- Push pins and noticeboard (if one is not provided).

Electrical.

- Laptop and chargers.
- Phone chargers.
- I-pad, kindle, and chargers.
- Small printer and ink (consider the price of new ink cartridges when shopping for cheap printers).
- USB sticks.
- Batteries.
- Headphones
- Adaptors, especially if you are an international student.

Documents.

- ID such as driving license or passport.
- National insurance number.

- Student ID number (SID).
- NHS medical card or health insurance for international students.
- Insurance details.
- Accommodation documents including a copy of your tenancy agreement/contract.
- Travel cards.
- Bank cards.

Moving home.

Moving out of the family home to start your student journey is both exciting and a little scary, not just for you, but your parents too. I have no doubt Mum has insisted she go with you to help you unpack and get set up in halls and most universities will be fine with this. It can be an emotional roller coaster for all members of the family.

Some institutions may allow you to park on campus for a short time to unpack your belongings and will send booking times in advance. It is worth planning the logistics of the move ahead of time.

Usually this will involve booking a date and time slot for parking, the institute should send out an automated reminder, but it may be worth contacting them if you have any concerns. In busy inner-city universities they may limit your parking for a set time to unload. Afterwards your parents would have to find parking nearby and return to help unpack.

You may find with many mums that despite the university deep cleaning each room, she will insist on giving the place a once over before she leaves. Humour her, as they say, "cleanliness is next to godliness" and with hundreds of rooms to clean in a short time, the cleaning crew may have missed a spot. In this instance it is perfectly fine to contact your housing manager and ask for the cleaners to return, but I understand that many people do not want to make a fuss and will handle it themselves.

Once you have moved in, met your new flat mates and after the family goes home, you can sometimes feel lost, alone, and out of your depth.

Remember to keep regular contact with the family, you can pre plan set times/dates for video calls for the first few days.

Although I suspect the pre-planned jelly shots and games night will help break the ice in the flat and you will be off enjoying your new life. You will soon forget about mum and dad but remember to drop them a line from time to time, they will appreciate it.

As mentioned previously, setting expectations is the key to ensuring a smoother transition into student accommodation life. Use the early days to have group meetings with your new flat mates, establish Rota's for cleaning and taking rubbish out and make sure everyone has equal space in shared cupboards and fridges.

Use this opportunity to cement your relationship with new flat mates, you do not want to be considered a tyrant, the bossy or nosy member of the flat, but you need to set out your expectations early, come to an understanding of how things should work and set rules even if that means compromising.

Budgeting.

You have planned your move to university, mum and dad have helped you unpack and settle into your new room, they have done your first big shop for you, but now you have to plan your budget for the coming year.

The following tips can help ensure you do not run out of money:

Write weekly meal plans: Set your budget, decide what to buy, then draw up a shopping list and do not deviate from it. Supermarkets are clever with marketing and have impulse aisles in places they know will attract you. Stay strong, stay on budget.

Get cashback on your shopping: There are many apps you can download that will give you money off your shopping, from Shopmium and Quidco ClickSnap that offer freebies at certain times of the year, to CheckoutSmart which offers cashback on alcohol and GreenJinn which is great for fruit and veg.

Get free stuff: I know, crazy right? companies will give you free stuff if you know how. Look online at sites such as **www.freestuff.co.uk**. If you have a kindle, you can download free from a range of books on amazon. By downloading the KFC app, you are given stamps that can be redeemed for popcorn chicken or hot wings.

Some restaurants will even let you eat free on your birthday, such as Frankie & Benny. You need to sign up to their rewards system and they send the voucher 10 days before your birthday. The caveat is that you must be with a paying customer, but if you and a friend both do it, you only pay once each for two meals out.

Greggs also offer a free cake or doughnut on your birthday by downloading their app, as do Krispy Kreme.

Mystery diner/pub tester: Sign up a mystery diner in your area, this will require you to document your experiences and send in reviews, which is time intensive, but you get to eat for free. Alternatively signing up as a pub tester means you can get paid for going to the pub and ensuring they check IDs.

Buy value brands and short date items: Supermarket own brands are fine for when you are budgeting, you can make a hefty saving by switching from named brands.

If you team up with flat mates you can buy wholesale which works out cheaper than buying independently from the supermarket.

Shopping in supermarkets such as Co-op can be cheaper as they offer a student discount (10%). Remember to ask in your regular shops if they take the Totum (student) card and get one ordered through the NUS (National Union of Students) as soon as possible.

Most supermarkets will reduce items that are reaching their sell by dates, a lot of items are perfectly fine to eat close to their end dates and you can make savings on regular purchases. You soon learn the best times of days to pick up reduced items.

Grow your own food/forage: You may not have access to an allotment or garden in your accommodation, but many locations, towns and cities in the UK do have them. By contacting the local council in advance, you may be able to get hold of an allotment nearby, and they are relatively cheap (some areas have waiting lists of years unfortunately). Not only is gardening really good for your mental health, but growing food can save you a lot of money, even better if you have others who can help on this project, and it can become a social experience and not a chore.

Of course, it is highly unlikely that most 18-year-olds will want to do this, but I hope a small proportion will. Alternatively starting small in this area could set you on a path to your own edible garden and food-scaping project later in life.

To experiment or start small, window boxes are great ways to grow herbs and salad greens in your accommodation, seeds and equipment can seem expensive, but there are ways to obtain free or cheap seeds:

- Set up a local seed circle, swap excess seeds with other students.
- Check the Student Union and sustainability groups for giveaways.
- Look online for free seeds, a quick google search shows me that the BBC and world-vision are giving away free seed packets at the time of writing. Check out **www.freestuff.co.uk** for more information.

You can recycle plastic ice cream tubs and other similar sized containers instead of buying pots and window boxes and you can also grow from kitchen waste rather than buying seeds.

When I say kitchen waste, I mean the things you normally do not eat and would throw away. A good example of this would be sprouting potatoes, taking these to the garden and burying them could generate 5-10 times as many potatoes later in the year, of course this assumes you have access to a garden and many students will not.

So, whilst potatoes are too large a plant to cultivate in a DIY window box, here are some that can:

Spring onions: When you cut the white root section off, try to leave around 3cm. put these in soil and once regrown you can cut them at the base of the plant and it will regrow, this can be done 3-4 times before the plant dies. If you do not have the soil/pot, you can use a glass jar and submerge around half the 'root' in water. Leave in a sunny area and change the water every second day.

Lettuce: This method works best with Romaine or Little Gem varieties. Cut the 'root' of the lettuce off, leaving at least 3cm of material at the root end. Place in a bowl of water to submerge the root to about 1cm depth. Leave in a sunny area and replace water every second day. After about two weeks new leaves should start to grow, you can then transplant this into a window box for better growth. Leaves can be harvested when they reach around 10cm.

Celery: Much like the process mentioned above, cutting the root section, and putting into a jar with water will allow the celery to regrow, when new leaves start to grow transplant into window box with soil.

Carrot tops: You cannot grow new carrots by planting the cut ends of a carrot, you can however, grow new carrot leaves which are high in vitamins C and K. Cut the top of the carrot leaving 2-3cm of 'top', leave it to dry in a cool dry area for 3-4 days.

Place the cutting in soil so that only the very top is exposed and leave in a sunny area, watering once the first 2-3cm of soil is dry. After 2-3 weeks you can harvest the green leaves.

Growing from seeds: Foods like tomatoes, peppers and chilli's come with seeds inside. These seeds can be harvested and used to grow new vegetables. Pulpy seeds like tomatoes can go mouldy if you do not remove the pulp first. You can dry them by putting them on paper towels for a week or so, dab the pulp away and change the paper towel when wet. Once you have dry seeds these can be planted in a window box in soil and watered regularly.

Herbs: Herbs can be grown from seeds or stem cuttings, if you know someone who has plants you can ask them for a few cuttings to start you off. You would need approximately 10cm of the herb plant cut below the node (where leaf grows from). You would then need to strip all leaves apart from the top 3-4 cm, place in a glass of water up to the leafy section and leave in direct sunlight. Roots will begin to grow and when you see signs of new leaf growth, they are ready to transplant into a pot of soil.

The UK wastes 4-5 million tonnes of food annually. And this food waste is a large cause of greenhouse gas emissions, we need to consider our relationship with our food not just for the financial costs. Growing food at home is good for the environment and great for your mental wellbeing.

If your fortunate enough to live in a greener area but do not want to grow your own food, there may be opportunity to forage for some food items. Taking a walk-through dense woodland, basket in hand, is a much harder thing to do for many city-based university students, but if you are close to forested areas, parks, and wild areas there can usually be some food sources on hand.

In the UK's woodlands and hedgerows, you are likely to find dandelions, roses, mushrooms, hawthorn leaves, nettles, garlic mustard, wild mint, and wild garlic. As well as berries such as blackberries, elderberries, or sloes

Obviously, I do not advocate scrumping or stealing from allotments and people's gardens, it is also illegal to dig up and remove plants without permissions from landowners, but foraging (removing fruits and leaves for food) is legal, in the vast majority of UK spaces.

Foraging can be as difficult as you want it to be, to keep it simple, keep to safe plants you recognise, blackberries and dandelions, rose-hips etc, but other edibles can be identified with a little bit of research such as wild mint. Mushrooms however can be dangerous without knowing what you are picking, as many species are poisonous to humans.

There are a lot of resources available to learn more on foraging, from online groups, survivalists and so on.

If in doubt regarding foraging, speak to local growers at allotments and food gardens, they may be happy for you to take some excess food.

There are many other ways to reduce your outgoings at university, some people get part time jobs in restaurants, which offer free meals on working days. Choosing larger meals, and then wrapping up leftovers to take home is a great way to save on food.

The best advice I can give is to reduce your outgoings through non-essential purchases. Give up take-aways by learning to cook cheap meals at home, give up smoking and daily costa coffee purchases, instead invest in a travel mug and bring coffee with you from home in the mornings.

I realise for many people planning to attend university, a lot of this will be daunting, most of you will need to get part time jobs to make ends meet, even with these saving tips.

Later in this book I will discuss ways to cope with stress, and time management in addition to a myriad of other concerns and potential issues.

Cooking on a budget.

A big secret to cooking on a budget is to manage food waste, I have already mentioned having pre-set meal plans and writing strict shopping lists to avoid buying unnecessary food, however, what you will find is that you will generate a lot of leftovers, especially when cooking for one. By learning to use these leftover foods, you can save a lot of money in the long term.

The two main methods to use leftovers I would advise are the breakfast burrito and rice/pasta meals:

Breakfast burrito: As the name suggests, having a few spare wraps on hand can be useful for making a meal from next to nothing. Traditionally scrambled eggs are the main ingredient in a breakfast burrito, and to this you would add any onions, green vegetables, and tomatoes you had laying around. But honestly you can put anything into a wrap: Cheese, bacon, avocado even a veggie wrap. The key to this is to freeze some spare tortilla wraps and defrost one or two at a time, many leftover foods can be frozen too.

Wraps are a great way to use leftovers at lunchtimes too, leftover chicken from a roast makes a great lunch time treat.

Rice/pasta meals: Anything can go well with these staple foods, want to make a bolognaise with leftover tuna, its surprisingly good. You can make a pasta bake with breadcrumbs from bread that is starting to go stale, mixing it with a little grated cheese and topping part cooked pasta that is mixed with tomatoes (works with tinned baked beans too). Cook it in the oven for 20 mins and you have a great tasting meal.

Other enjoyable meals can include a vegetable chilli or vegetable curry, both made from leftovers and made better if you have some beans, chickpeas, or lentils on hand.

There is a valid reason survivalists harp on about rice and beans, it contains all the calories and protein you may need (if not a little tasteless and boring). I am not suggesting you all eat rice and beans, however, there is some sound advice here.

Firstly, ensure you have a healthy supply of staple foods like rice and pasta, its relatively cheap especially if you buy in bulk, and secondly food items such as beans, lentils and pulses are a far cheaper protein source than meat. And whilst I would not advocate people become vegetarian/vegan to help with budget, perhaps establishing meat free Mondays would be a good way to save a little money.

Eating cheaply could be as simple as half a tin of baked beans with pasta, throwing in a leftover sausage or chorizo cut up into pieces can make it much tastier.

The other half of the tin can be used for baked beans on toast for breakfast the following morning. And if you are toasting it, the bread does not have to be high quality, you can get away with cheap branded bread instead.

When shopping for foods, have a look for cheaper items such as 'wonky vegetables' and the aforementioned reduced, end of life foods.
UHT milk whilst not as appetising will last much longer than fresh and reduce wastage.

Alternatively adapting to having tea and coffee black is a good way to save on buying milk.

Another way to combat food waste, is to store foods correctly to ensure they last longer. Outside of the obvious items, such as milk belonging in the fridge, some good examples of knowing the best methods of storage are as follows:

- Apples: Will stay fresh for longer when stored in the fridge rather than a fruit bowl.
- Eggs: best stored in the fridge.
- Bananas: Storing in a cool dry cupboard will ensure they last longer than the fruit bowl, these will go black very quickly if refrigerated.
- Onions: best stored in a cupboard, ideally in a cloth bag away from sunlight. Spring onions should be refrigerated.

One final thought I would share here is that cooking for two is not much more expensive than cooking for one, you leave less food waste. By alternating cooking evenings with flat mates, you can all save a little money on the weekly shop.

Health.

There are many issues you are likely to face in halls. It is likely in the first two weeks student life will come at you fast, fresher's week, meeting new people and new experiences, late night parties and drunken hook-ups. Going to class, meeting your classmates and teachers, and growing into new routines.

After the second or third week many students find a sense of homesickness start to creep in, much like a fresher's hangover after the excitement dies down. This can also be accompanied by (and can in part cause) 'freshers' flu', a severe cold like illness that can make you feel rubbish for a week or two.

Fresher's flu is brought on by a mixture of physical and psychological factors that hammer away at your immune system.

Firstly, you will be mixing with people from all over the country and indeed, world. Who will likely have viruses that your immune system is not used to.

Thankfully, the recent experience with coronavirus gives us valuable experience in tackling the spread of viruses: Social distancing and antibacterial hand gel (washing hands frequently) are a good start, however if we are being honest, asking students to distance from each other is like asking a fire not to burn!

The second factor is lack of sleep, with fresher's week, partying, late night drinks with flat mates, and early rises for class you are burning the candle at both ends. Remember to give yourself some time to recover, the odd early night and/or lay in is good for you.

The next reason is diet: junk food and takeaways are more convenient than cooking, especially when preparing and cooking meals means less time with new friends going shot for shot, of course too much alcohol will also reduce your body's natural defence against viruses. You will find in time that self-care is an important aspect of adapting to student life, I will discuss self-care in more detail later.

Lastly is stress: new environments, worried about making friends, new classes and being homesick puts a psychological pressure on your body.

These combined factors really do a number on your immune system and as you may have realised, there is not a lot you can do to avoid many of these without impacting your own experience.

On a more serious note, all the reasons above combined with student proximity in halls makes students the most 'at risk' group for certain illnesses. The most concerning is meningitis, the most aggressive strain 'Men W' can cause serious symptoms which can include inflammation in the lining of the brain and if not diagnosed and treated early enough can result in death.

Thankfully, it is still considered a rare occurrence, although rates have increased over the last decade. It is important to look out for the following symptoms and seek medical attention as soon as possible:

- Stiff neck
- Severe headache
- Photophobia or light sensitivity

- High temperature
- Vomiting
- Rash

The rash will begin by looking like tiny pinpricks, but eventually turns into purple blotches. If pressing on the rash with a glass tumbler does not make them fade, its likely meningitis.

As you may have already surmised, many of these symptoms are present with a hangover, drug use or even fresher's flu. Keep watch for the photophobia and the rash, these are key symptoms which should not be ignored and call 999 if you have any concerns, even without these two symptoms.

Speak to your family doctor to see if you are eligible for a Meningitis vaccination prior to moving into halls.

Another illness to watch for is Glandular fever (often call the kissing disease), it presents with flu like symptoms, swollen tonsils, swollen glands in the arm pit and groin and a sore throat. Thankfully once you have had it, you are immune to reinfection.

An additional illness to be aware of is Legionnaires disease; a severe form of pneumonia or lung inflammation, caused by a bacteria known as legionella (legionella pneumophilia). It can be caught by inhaling bacteria from water, usually aerosolised water from showers and from drinking water

Not everyone exposed will become sick but people with weakened immune systems and smokers are more susceptible and if untreated it can be fatal. Symptoms include a high fever (40c or higher), muscle and headaches. Further symptoms develop shortly after and may include cough with mucus and/or blood, chest pain, nausea, diarrhoea, and vomiting.

Legionella tends to multiply in human made water systems, and whilst it is possible to see it in home plumbing, its far more likely to exist in larger buildings such as student accommodation. This is due to large scale; complex plumbing works allowing the bacteria to spread and multiply.

Building owners and landlords have legal obligations under sections 2 & 3 of the health and safety at work act (1974), the control of substances hazardous to health regulation (1994) and approved code of practice L8, to monitor all water sources.

Taps, shower heads etc will be tested regularly by the university, or approved contractor. If any signs of bacteria are present, the areas will be professionally cleaned and flushed to prevent anyone from getting sick.

To prepare for the sudden shock of student life to your immune system, it would be beneficial to prepare a balanced meal plan to ensure you have the correct nutrients and vitamins. Given the likelihood of this happening and bearing in mind student finances do not often stretch to fresh fish, meats, and fresh vegetables (pot noodle anyone?), immune system boosting multi vitamins can prove useful and these can be pre-packed prior to moving in.

Other means of helping your immune system naturally are:

- Giving up smoking: as an additional benefit, you will likely live years longer as a result, and save money.

- Good hygiene: to remove nasty bacteria from yourself and surroundings, both self-care and ventilating and cleaning your room helps.

Whilst I have covered the physical factors affecting health, the psychological aspects of wellbeing must also be addressed, whilst I will discuss mental health in greater detail later, there are a few things you can do to prepare yourself for life as a student.

Let consider homesickness first; there are things you can do to mitigate feelings of the unfamiliar. Stay connected with home by regularly speaking with friends and family, as much as you miss them, they will miss you too and regular contact will benefit everyone. Also stay connected to your home and family by bringing keepsakes and memories with you. Furnish your room with pictures that remind you of home; just remember that not all institutes allow you to stick pictures to bare walls, they may provide your own pin board or area for such, just remember to read your tenancy agreement before you arrive.

Whilst your room may be your 'safe space' getting outside and into nature can really help, as can exercise. By exploring the campus, surrounding areas, and meeting new people you begin to make the area familiar, and the sense of homesickness may go away naturally as the university becomes your new home. Meditation and yoga can also be useful for relaxing albeit it may be a little kitsch and not for everyone.

Pressure and stress of studies is another issue to consider, with the combined living costs and accommodation being more than student loans means you may have to have a part time job to help pay for food and other necessary items.

Creating a healthy work/life balance and managing your time are key skills. As someone who is currently juggling a family, career, degree and drafting this book my advice is to plan your time efficiently, you will undoubtedly have to make sacrifices, but you must prioritise your needs.

Create a schedule or planner at the start of each semester. Note submission dates for essays and plan in writing time and time for feedback changes to submissions, break up your work into manageable blocks and do not leave until tomorrow what you can achieve today.

Study during daylight hours, for each hour spent studying during the day you would have to spend an hour and a half at night. In most cases the classes for university students are not back-to-back Monday to Friday as they are during A-levels, you do get free (study) time and even free days.

By studying and writing assignments on weekdays, it frees up evenings and weekends for working and spending time with friends. By studying during the day, you can ensure you are well rested and can concentrate more.

Take regular small breaks, try not to overload yourself, work 45 minutes every hour, then make a cup of tea. More importantly remove distractions, for the 45-minute blocks you work, put your phone on silent and out of arms reach, check it on the break and then put it down and start again.

Fulfil the objectives for the day, then reward yourself with personal time or drinks with friends. Meeting goals reduces stress as you do not feel like your falling behind. People will feel stressed by falling behind and to relieve the stress will go out to chill/relax with friends but will then feel they have wasted more time by going out and this will exacerbate the feelings of stress.

Student experiences.

There are a diverse range of options for student accommodation, around a third of students live in university accommodation, whilst half live in the private sector, a further one in ten students live in privately owned halls.

The university experience is seemingly good for the majority, however around a third of all students do not feel they are getting value for money. Almost half struggle to pay their rent, almost half say their accommodation impacts their mental health and around a third say it affects their studies too.

Whilst two thirds of institutes offer all-inclusive rent, others do not. It is important to determine what your rent payment covers before you can budget your limited finances.

Whilst most students are overall happy with their student experience, stressful situations can occur. According to the 2022 national student accommodation survey the following were issues for students in accommodation:

- Noisy housemates (52%)
- Damp (38%)
- Housemates stealing food (37%)
- Lack of water/heating (34%)
- Disruptive building work (22%)
- Rodents and pests (18%)
- Inappropriate landlord visits (14%)
- Dangerous living conditions (8%)

- Break in or burglary (6%)
- Bed bugs (4%)

Of course, Some horror stories do stand out from within the industry, from a flatmate defecating on the kitchen floor to drug dealing in halls, but thankfully these are rare anecdotes. In my personal experience the main causes of issues are usually flatmates refusing to clean, being too loud and disruptive or inter-flat conflict due to a multitude of personal reasons.

Most institutes sign up to the Universities UK, accommodation code of practice (ACOP). This code was developed in cooperation between a wide range of organisations, to create a set of good practices for the management of student accommodation and to ensure compliance with the housing act 2004. Even if the institute is not a member of ACOP they must still abide by UK laws in the services it offers.

It is a wide-ranging policy but in simple terms by law, institutes must provide you the following:

- Healthy, safe environment.
- Timely repairs and maintenance.
- Clean pleasant living environment.
- Formal, contractual relationship with your landlord.
- Access to health and wellbeing services.
- A living environment, free from anti-social behaviour.

Some of these issues may seem vague, what does timely mean? What does pleasant mean? What is anti-social behaviour? If you have any doubts, you can view the full accommodation code of practice and housing act 2004 online to determine what the institutes responsibilities are to resolve your situation. Furthermore, tenancy agreements should have a section on the responsibilities of your landlords, and you can ask for a copy of this at any time from your institute. It always pays to ask for a copy at the time of signing, some institutes will provide you a blank copy when you book your room.

Lockouts:

By far the most common issue I have dealt with in housing management is students getting locked out of their rooms, the reasons are usually similar: "left my key in the room, went to make a cup of tea" etc.

Many halls/accommodations will operate a front desk, 24-hour cover or a system of out of hours contacts such as residential assistants and on call managers. I personally use residential assistants, a team of student staff who hold an emergency phone out of hours for emergency contact purposes.

Check what system your institute uses and take down any relevant contact numbers, if you lose your key or get locked out, you will not have to crash on a friend's couch for the night, you can be let back into your room with the minimum of fuss.

Please be aware however, that some institutes may charge for these services, and repeated lockouts could become costly. Find a way to remind yourself about keys before leaving your room, many students I have dealt with put signs on the back of their doors, so they do not make the same mistake.

If you do get locked out and do not have your phone on you, the contact numbers should be on posters in communal areas, you could knock for neighbours to help you make a phone call or go to security/front desk who can contact the out of hours number for you.

Noisy housemates:

This is a common complaint we see in student accommodation. There are usually rules regarding noise built into student tenancy agreements, be sure to check the details when you read through, it will read something akin to the following:

"The Tenant must not annoy or cause a nuisance or danger to other tenants or neighbours. The Tenant must not organise or allow parties or other social gatherings which are likely to cause too much noise or nuisance, in the boundaries of the Property or Building or grounds."

Note in the example given it does not ban parties/gatherings per se, only parties or gatherings that will cause too much noise. Also consider that students will be held liable for any guests, their behaviour, and any rules violations. So, if you have loud friends, might be best to avoid having them over at midnight for a drink and catch up.

When planning for your stay in halls, find out the best places for large gatherings, birthday parties and social events. Is there a common room or student union area that can be used in the late evenings? This is a good question to ask at open days.

Generally flat mates will not mind you are having some friends over in the early evenings for pre drinks, maybe even playing music. However, once you get to a reasonable hour, around 10-11pm the noise needs to be at a more respectable level. Also consider reciprocating, if you are having friends over on occasion, you need to tolerate when your flat mates do it too.

Setting expectations and following agreed flat rules is key to a stress-free experience but if you are following flat rules and someone else is not, things can spiral out of control very quickly.

Just like the initial conversations in setting expectations and flat rules, initial breaches of rules should be resolved with a quiet word. Waiting until you are frustrated and emotional and leaving passive aggressive notes could potentially lead to conflict.

Early communication is important to achieve a peaceful resolution, make them aware of the issue, be calm and see it as a friendly chat and not a confrontation, they may not realise they are making too much noise and will be more considerate in future.

Alternatively, if it is a one off, it is their birthday or other special event, it might be worth shutting it out, use the opportunity to go to the library and study or spend the evening at a friend's place, knowing your flat mate would be willing to do the same for you.

If the quiet word fails or the behaviour occurs frequently it becomes necessary to seek other means of resolution via the building management team, but you need to consider the consequences of any actions you take, it is easy to escalate a small issue into real conflict.

Damp:

There are four main causes of damp in a building: Rising damp, Penetrating damp, internal leaks, and condensation.

Rising damp occurs when the property is built without an appropriate damp proof course, or it is defective and damp transfers from the ground into low levels of the walls. Penetrating damp occurs due to water ingress because of structural defects, most commonly faulty guttering, or damaged roofing.

These types of issues may be prevalent in older houses and could be an issue if you are renting in the private sector or university managed leased houses, these damp issues should be reported to your landlord or building manager as a matter of urgency.
If you are living in student halls, its more common for damp to be because of a leak or condensation.

Leaks can be a common risk in halls, especially if you consider the amount of pipe-work present. Older halls that have a lot of past repairs and refurbishments will have dead ends or dog legs that can cause further issues, from weak points to slow drainage. Drainage issues can cause your ensuite shower to overflow and flood your room, damaging walls, carpets and increasing moisture in the air causing mould.

The most common damp issue to face students will be condensation, especially in ensuite rooms. With small, enclosed spaces and poor ventilation a hot shower will cause a lot of condensation, this will, if not dealt with cause mould problems on the walls and ceilings of your ensuite bathrooms.

Condensation (and mould) can form on any surface that changes temperature regularly, boiling kettles and cooking can cause the issue in kitchens, usually around windows, whereas drying clothes and hot showers will cause issues in your room.

To control condensation in the kitchen, open windows, and close doors when cooking (usually a fire regulation anyway) and use lids on saucepans to reduce steam, try to keep windows open for at least 20 minutes after cooking and wipe away any condensation that forms on walls and windows.

In rooms, avoid drying clothes on radiators, the water evaporates and turns into moisture in the air, too much moisture will cause damp on the walls, which in turn can develop into black mould. This mould has the potential to cause respiratory problems from spores that you breathe in but can also damage and stain walls that you could be held liable for.

If you have the ability, drying clothes on a washing line is preferable, but that depends on your living situation. If you are in halls, you will not have that option, but you should have access to a laundrette for washing and drying clothes. If you absolutely must dry clothes indoors, make sure to do so in a well-ventilated room, open the window and avoid covering radiators. You should never cover an electric radiator as this is a serious fire hazard.

To prevent hot showers resulting in damp and black mould growth, ensure there is adequate ventilation, after your shower ensure the door or window is left open so moisture does not build up. Make sure to wipe down surfaces of any moisture that does appear and clean regularly to avoid black mould.

If black mould does start to grow you can use a mould and mildew remover, available from most local supermarkets or DIY stores. Alternatively diluting bleach with hot water can be effective, just be sure to use the correct PPE (Personal Protective Equipment), such as gloves and masks, scrub the affected area and dry the area after to avoid regrowth.

For large scale black mould colonies, report these as a matter of urgency as touching it can result in the release of spores that may be harmful to your health. However, if the mould growth is a result of your own negligence, then you may be held liable for any professional cleaning costs, this is still preferable to becoming ill because of tackling it yourself, however.

If there is rising, penetrating damp or it is a result of a leak, the institute has an obligation to set this right to provide a healthy, safe environment and should commence repairs in a timely manner.

Please remember that housing managers are not mind readers or clairvoyants, if you do not report issues, they cannot resolve them. Any repairs will be measured from the time of the first report for dealing with complaints if you feel they were not timely.

Fire sensors in room:

Every student's room will be fitted with a fire sensor, these are incredibly sensitive and ensure the safety of all students in halls.
It is common for the fire alarm to be set off due to steam from a shower or someone spraying deodorant underneath the sensor.

I am acutely aware that in larger halls frequent fire alarm activations causes a lot of frustration among the students, the advice I give is to avoid spraying deodorant or aerosols under the sensor and to ventilate well after a shower (open doors and windows).

What you should not do is to cover the fire sensors. For any reason!

It is common among those who smoke in their rooms to cover the sensors with a plastic bag or a sock, not only is this a serious breach of your tenancy agreement (as is smoking in room), but it can also cause faults in the sensor which in cases of real emergencies can risk the life of you and others.

Many institutes will have a different approach to this issue. For myself, I take the safety of students very seriously, if someone covers a fire sensor, I will always have it tested and the costs recharged to the student responsible. In addition to this I will take disciplinary action against the student.

For your own safety and the safety of others, do not tamper with firefighting equipment, this also includes fire extinguishers and fire blankets. I unfortunately see occurrences of students setting fire extinguishers off in halls, by misusing these items they put everyone at risk.

If students are caught discharging extinguishers, they will be asked to cover the cost of replacement, and the new P50 all use extinguishers are very expensive.

Fire doors are also an important part of student accommodation. They are designed to be secure for 30 mins within a fire to slow its spread throughout the building. However, it can only do its job if it is kept closed.

Fire doors should be kept closed where possible especially if you leave the area or are cooking.

Do not prop open fire doors, you could be putting others at risk.

<u>Television licensing.</u>

The requirement for a TV license is mandated by the communications act 2003, specifically section 363.

The law currently says that you need a license to:

- Watch or record programmes as they are being shown on TV, on any channel.
- Download or watch BBC programmes through BBC iPlayer.
- Watch or stream programmes live on an online TV service such as YouTube, amazon prime, ITV hub, Now TV etc.

License is mandatory regardless of what device you use to stream or watch live TV, whether that be your laptop, tablet, or iPhone. To simplify if you watch any live TV via any means or watch any on demand services from BBC you need a license. You would not need one for watching YouTube videos, but if you watch sky news live via YouTube you would, as it is being broadcast live. This includes watching non-UK channels live.

An on-demand programme is anything that can be downloaded that is not being broadcast live on TV, for example Netflix movies.

I must be very careful what I say here, as my own bias is very anti-license fee. In my defence that is the general feeling amongst most people I know. The current government has promised to scrap the fee by 2027, although I personally do not trust politicians.

Until 2027 however the legal requirement is still in place and if asked if students need a license the general advice is always to refer to the legislation.

Given the current GDPR regulations, the TV licensing authorities have no way to know who you are unless you tell them. Nor do they know if you are watching live TV. The university will not be able or willing to give your details to them either.

I am intentionally not finishing my line of thought there, as the law is the law and if you watch live TV, you need to have purchased a license.

Housemates stealing food:

Moving in with a diverse group of people can be challenging, I have spoken a few times already about the importance of communicating with flat mates and setting expectations. Everyone should have their own cupboard and fridge space and feel included in the shared areas, most institutes will include lockable cupboards in kitchens for each student, depending on your living situation. Despite this, it is common to find small amounts of food will disappear from your part of the fridge overnight.

This can be someone "borrowing" milk and cheese as theirs runs out but can also be a drunk or stoned flat mate with midnight munchies not respecting your boundaries.

When visiting halls on open days, enquire about fridges in your room, some halls do not allow them, some provide them, but clearly having your own private space will prevent food theft. If you have severe dietary issues, allergies or medicines, institutes will likely provide or allow you to bring mini fridges for your room. Speak to the residential team to confirm and discuss these issues before you move in.

Outside of these options, sharing fridges may be unavoidable and you may lose the odd food item. There are three choices open to you, you can accept the loss, write it off and only buy small amounts at a time to mitigate your losses. You can try to resolve issues within the flat, sometimes the guilty party will admit it and offer to replace your items, other times assuming you were not overly abrasive during the flat meeting, the guilty party will realise they have ben rumbled and may not do it again. Finally, if all else fails you can report the matter to the housing manager, as it is technically theft.

The odds of finding the guilty party if they choose not to admit fault are low, but it does put everyone in the flat on notice and people will start playing detective, flat mates being more aware will reduce the likelihood of repeat occurrences.

Fridge/Freezers:

One of the other causes of 'lost' food is issues with fridge freezers frosting over. When this occurs, the ice builds up and you cannot shut the door properly, as a result food items in the fridge go bad. Usually, you find you cannot get items from the freezer as the drawers are frosted shut and trying to use force means you break the plastic drawers.

This problem is quite common in student accommodation and can be caused by the following issues:

- Humidity: Every time you open the freezer door, cold air escapes and warm air enters, the humidity of the warm air will condense and freeze. In halls with shared freezers, the frequency of opening and closing of the freezer door can be a factor in over frosting. When you hover with the door open for long periods this can exacerbate the issue further. Reduce this issue by labelling your foods and having a manageable storing system.

- Freezing hot food: A further issue introducing humidity into the freezer, wait for hot food to cool to room temperature before putting in the freezer.

- Temperature settings: Setting the dial too high or low can cause frost build up, the ideal temperature for a freezer is -18 degrees. Check the thermometer regularly.

- Wet food: when you introduce moisture to a freezer, you introduce ice, make sure everything is dried off before storing.

- Door seal: If the freezer door seal is damaged or worn, this will cause warm air to enter (humidity), check with your landlord or building manager to have the seal replaced.

If you find your freezer has iced over, you should attempt to manually defrost it using the following method:
- Switch off the freezer
- Prepare the surrounding area, put old towels down to soak up water, or be prepared to mop regularly throughout the day.

- Remove food and store elsewhere, if possible. Student halls generally have multiple fridge freezers, normally 1 for every 4 students who share the kitchen. You may have problems if the drawers are stuck together, try not to damage drawers as you may be held accountable for replacement costs.
- Wait for the ice to melt, this will take a few hours, I usually recommend waiting overnight.
- Clean out the fridge freezer, its empty so what better opportunity to clean that weird unidentified goop at the bottom of the fridge.
- Dry the fridge freezer with a hand towel. Any moisture left from the defrost or cleaning will turn into ice again.
- Switch back on and allow a few hours for temperature to settle before using again.

If this process is followed and the freezer frosts over right away, it may be an issue with the unit itself, perhaps even a damaged seal. You should report this to the housing management team as soon as possible.

Lack of water/heating:

There are multiple reasons for a sudden loss of water, hot water, or heating, this could be a local outage due to a leak or repair of an underground pipe. In this instance your local water board should put out notifications on social media, google is your friend.

If it is just hot water and heating that's out, but cold water still comes through its likely to be a fault with the boiler. In this case contact your landlord or building manager, who is responsible for providing a healthy, safe environment and timely repairs and maintenance.

Bearing in mind of course that boiler maintenance is a specialised task which may require an external engineer who can take time to organise and attend.

Speak with the landlord or manager who should be able to provide a temporary heater and may suggest an alternate place to shower in the short term.

With a lot of institutes now focussed on being environmentally friendly, you may find that heating is only on at certain times of the day depending on the time of year. You can enquire with your housing manager about this if you are frequently cold, but having an extra blanket on hand, especially during winter months can make you feel more comfortable.

As a housing manager myself, I find heating to be a contentious issue among houses of mixed cultural backgrounds. Most UK born students are comfortable within houses, even with environmental/green limitations. I have found individuals from other countries however, like having their rooms so hot, you could cook an egg on the desk.

The hope is that through acclimatisation these students can eventually learn to deal with colder UK temperatures. In the meantime, a conversation within the house about compromise may be in order. It is better that one person must wear a sweater, than another is uncomfortably hot. And more environmentally friendly too.

Trip Switches:

Also known as circuit breakers or RCDs, trip switches are essentially fuses that break the circuit when too much load is passed through the electrical system.

The most common reasons for 'trips' are:

- Damaged plugs or cables.

- Overloading circuits with too many items: Plugging too many items into extension leads etc, also note that daisy chaining would be considered overloading, but also becomes a fire risk. Daisy chaining is plugging an extension lead into another extension lead.

- Faulty appliances, this can include foreign and cheap made products, I regularly deal with Chinese made 'amazon' chargers and rice cookers. If you must buy from amazon, buy UK made, branded products to avoid this issue.

- Water ingress: water conducts electricity and if it finds its way into a socket it will cause the system to short. Legally speaking outlets should be a minimum distance from sinks and water sources to prevent this, but splashes, cooking and water leaks can cause water ingress.

If a system is reset and trips additional times, it indicates there is a deeper issue that needs fixing, and this should be reported to your landlord or building manager.

In many halls of residence, access to distribution boards (consumer units) will be limited for students, they may be locked or in hard to access cupboards. However, in shared houses you will probably find a distribution board under the stairs or in a cupboard.

If a switch has tripped, please contact the out of hours number to arrange an electrician to attend. Please be aware that anything considered non urgent may not be addressed until the next working day. However, issues like heating (during winter), food and medicine storage (fridges, freezers etc) would be considered urgent.

PAT testing:

Portable appliance testing (PAT) is the inspection of electrical appliances to ensure they are safe to use. This is a legal requirement covered by the Electricity at Work Act 1989, although are no specific clauses on how often items are tested.

Whilst student accommodation providers and landlords are not legally obliged to carry out testing, they do have a requirement to ensure all electrical items on the premises are in safe working order and not a risk to health, a clever catch 22 which ensures they will carry out PAT testing.

Some institutions will organise their own PAT testing and schedule your room to be inspected within the first month of you moving in. The advice given is to put electrical items on display (on bed or desk) as the engineers/electricians would not want to search through your personal belongings.

Other institutions may insist you organise your own PAT testing prior to arrival on campus.

Disruptive building work:

Most universities will have an ongoing refurbishment and regeneration plan, some buildings will be demolished to make way for new modern buildings more suitable for today's teaching methods and technology.

Whilst this is undoubtedly a good thing, the building process itself can be distracting. From eye sore building sites to the disruptive noises of power tools.

These building projects should be obvious during site visits and open days, ask questions about completion dates and establish if they could cause potential disruption to your student experience. Should you be staying in a different location/hall or a different institute?

The most common form of disruption will come because of ongoing repair works within your halls, flat or house. With the institute responsible for you having a healthy, safe environment they will likely have onsite maintenance staff or responsible contractors.

For planned works, the institute should give you notice in advance, usually 7 days, usually by email. If they give you advance notice, you cannot stop them from gaining access. This is something that usually appears on your tenancy agreement:

"The Tenant must give access to the Landlord and the Landlord's representatives, when necessary, at all reasonable times".

What this means however is you have a week to tidy up, and if necessary, make plans to study in the library if your concerned about being disturbed.

One important caveat you need to be aware of is that whilst the building manager/landlord has responsibilities to make sure you have a healthy, safe environment and to effect repairs in a timely manner. You also have responsibilities to those working in your flat/house, this means you must ensure there are no trip, fire, electrical or other safety hazards, and to ensure your room is clean, tidy and pest free.

Rodents and pests:

Rats are a frequent issue in student accommodation. They are attracted by the sheer number of people, this increase in student numbers means more food, more food waste, and an abundance of food sources and shelter to rats in a small geographic area.

Rats vastly outnumber humans, and, in the UK, the most common type of rat is the brown rat, the largest of the species. They are distinguishable usually by size, but a black rat has a longer tail than its body, whereas a brown rat will not. The black rat tends to live around docklands and are increasingly rare in the UK, if you see a rat, chances are it is a "Ratticus Norvegicus" a brown rat.

Each female rat can reproduce every six weeks with litters of 6-8 pups in optimal conditions. Despite only living for one to two years, they are sexually mature at five weeks old and reproduce exponentially if there is adequate food.

Rats' incisor teeth continuously grow, and they constantly gnaw to wear them down, they will damage cables, pipework even bricks and can chew their way into waste pipes and create ingress points into buildings.

They are nocturnal and tend to live underground, usually in sewer access points. Although it is common to find them in roof spaces, wall cavities and even under floors. They come above ground to eat, find nesting materials and to breed/give birth.

There are multiple good reasons to control the spread of rats, firstly is the risk of disease. Rats spread Leptospirosis, salmonella, and listeria among other nasty diseases by urinating everywhere they go, whether that be work surfaces, in cupboards containing pots, pans and food prep equipment, or even on drinks cans (wash them prior to drinking and decant into a glass).

The second reason for controlling rats is the damage they can cause; it is estimated that 25% of all house fires started due to faulty wiring are a result of rats chewing through those wires. Rats can cause flooding by chewing through water pipes and can even chew through gas pipes causing harm to unsuspecting homeowners.

Rats are also responsible for damaging one fifth of the global food supply every year, at an estimated cost of £11 billion annually.

The presence of rats can be determined by gnaw marks, the presence of droppings (each rat can leave 40 droppings per night, usually clustered together), smear marks (dirty grease marks where the rub against surfaces) and sometimes even a unique unpleasant smell. The sounds of gnawing and scuttling around late at night are also clear evidence (although it may be squirrels and nesting pigeons).

Further examples of pests include wasps, ants, Mice, cockroaches, and pigeons, among others.

To prevent pests, you should consider the following:

- Report any gaps around water pipes, vents, windows or any other egress points to the property, rats only need a gap of 15mm despite their size.

- Report any nesting sites in the gardens, overgrown areas should be cut back, check with your landlord and tenancy agreement to see who carries the responsibility for this.

- Report any damaged or non-fitting drain covers.

- Cover household waste, ensure bin lids are closed and now waste is left in bags on the ground.

- Store opened food in sealed containers.

- Do not dump food waste directly into bins, package/wrap it first.

If you find evidence of rats, report this to your landlord or housing manager as soon as possible. Landlords and property owners have a legal obligation to keep premises rodent and pest free under the 'Prevention of damage by pests act 1949'. And this is enforced by local authorities. If landlords do not act on this issue, you can report directly to the local authorities (council) who can take legal action.

University institutes should have pest control procedures in place, perhaps even a contract with a professional pest control company. Once a problem is identified it is not a simple fix to resolve however and you must be patient.

Pest control specialists will usually locate egress and ingress points to the building, will lay traps and poisons near to nests, which will need to be monitored with further visits. This comprehensive approach will normally guarantee the issue is resolved, although it may take a few weeks to solve the problem entirely, depending on the pest.

One unpleasant issue with controlling rats, is that the dead carcasses emit a strong smell, if the pest control find these bodies they will remove them, but it is common for rats to crawl into tiny spaces before dying. And the smell can last for a few weeks. Pest control may have to make additional visits to your house/flat to change bait and check traps.

Bed bugs:

Like rodents and pests, the institute or landlord (if you rent privately) have a duty to arrange pest removal experts.

Bed bugs are a variety of dark yellow, red, or brownish in colour, adults are around 4-5mm long, they can avoid detection and survive months between feeding, and they reproduce quickly.

They tend to bite exposed areas whilst you are sleeping: the neck, face, and arms. These bites cause inflamed red spots that are itchy, and bites are usually in groups or lines in the same areas. Occasionally you may see spots of blood on the bed linen from the bites or from squashing a recently gorged bed bug.

Bed bugs are known for living in/on mattresses (hence the name) however they tend to hide in bed frames, folds in mattresses, in clothing, pictures, wallpaper and many more places, because of this bed bugs create a unique situation in that if present, housing managers cannot move the student from the room, or risk moving the infestation with them to the new room.

If bed bugs are present (housing managers may need to check to be sure), pest removal experts will be called who will treat the affected areas with insecticides, however this may take two to three weeks and multiple visits to completely clear. For a few hours after treatment, you will have to stay away from the room.

Until this can be organised, you can contain the infestation by hoovering the affected areas and possible hiding places, the mattress, bed frame, carpets, and curtains. Seal all your bed linen and clothes in plastic bags and wash them at high temperature as soon as possible. Pick up books, magazines, and anything else that is under your bed, throw out any rubbish and move your bed away from the wall or any other items of furniture.

Hoovering and changing bed linen will remove the worst of the offenders and you can monitor the issue until the pest removal expert can arrive and treat the room.

Bed bug bites tend to clear up on their own in around a week, keeping the affected skin clean and putting a cool damp cloth on the area can help with the itching and swelling. Try to avoid scratching as this can cause secondary infections. If you have reactions to bites, you may need to seek medical advice, a doctor may prescribe antihistamines or topical creams.

Guests and guest policy:

Whilst your flat mates may be ok with you having your boyfriend/girlfriend over every single night, you may be in breach of the university's rules.

In the institute in which I work, each room is allocated as single occupancy for reasons of fire safety, to ensure people are kept safe we instituted a "one night in seven" policy for overnight guests, with the understanding that these guests would also be made known to us in case of emergency.

Furthermore, personal experience tells me that flatmates are ok with something, until they are not. Sudden changes or a souring in relationships can change the way they view you having guests over, previously there were cool with it, but now they are not and have lodged a complaint about you.

It is always best to follow the rules of the university, to protect yourself from weaponised complaints. The argument of "my flat mates were ok with it before" is unfortunately not an adequate response to breaching your tenancy agreement.

Inappropriate landlord visits:

Whether you live in university managed halls or in a privately rented house the landlord has various rights and responsibilities, as do you the tenant. In terms of university managed accommodation, the university itself and its agents (housing management) can be considered the landlords.

One of the issues raised by students is that landlords can turn up with no notice and think they can access all parts of the property, this is not true.

A landlord should provide 24 hours' notice minimum, by writing (preferably email), of their intent to visit and then should visit during reasonable hours (office hours), universities often allow up to 7 days' notice for non-essential visits.

It is a criminal offence if your landlord behaves in a way that they believe may make you leave the property before you legally must, or makes you give up your tenancy rights.

This behaviour can include, but not limited to the following:

- Entering without permission.
- Threatening to change locks.
- Hiding, opening, or stealing your post.
- Interfering with or stealing personal property.
- Unfairly cutting off water, electricity, or heating without good reason (such as maintenance).
- Demands you pay money you do not owe. Landlords may contact you to discuss rent arrears, but this can never be an excuse to threaten eviction, nor can they turn up at the house demanding money.

General intimidating or threatening behaviour would also be covered, as would pressurising you to leave your tenancy early. Any discrimination you suffer because of your immutable characteristics (Race, gender, sexual preference etc) would be a further breach of the equalities act.

If you have concerns about your landlord visiting at inappropriate times you should contact your university, they may be able to speak with the landlord, offer legal advice or even relocate you should your safety be at risk.

Alternatively, you can speak with your local citizens advice bureau for legal advice or contact the organisation 'shelter' if you live in England or Scotland.

Shelter are a charity funded organisation who aim to ensure all tenants' rights are upheld and can provide legal advice or act on your behalf. The shelter website has good advice on dealing with rogue landlords, including among others a template letter to send in the first instances of landlords breaching the regulations.

I found this letter template very useful, so have included here:

[Edit writing in bold to your specific details.]

To **HMO manager name/landlord**

I am writing about your unannounced visits to **address.**

I am concerned that you are visiting my home without good reason and entering my room without permission.

I have a tenancy for my room and a lock on my door. You should only enter my room with my express permission.

You have no reason to come into my room unless I have reported a repair, or you have arranged an inspection.

You must give me at least 24 hours' written notice if you wish to inspect the condition of the room and can only visit at reasonable time of the day.

You must tell me when and why you intend to visit so I can confirm it is convenient and arrange to be there if a want to.

I accept that you may need to visit the property to show vacant rooms to other tenants and that you retain access to the shared areas.

However, you must not use this as an excuse to linger at the property, enter bedrooms uninvited or harass myself or other tenants whilst you are here.

Your actions may also constitute harassment under the 'Protection from Eviction Act 1977. This is a criminal offence.

I will consider reporting you to the local council for enforcement action if your behaviour continues.

Please only communicate with me by email in future.

Your name

Your email

Tenant rights:

Understanding your basic tenancy rights is important if you are going to live in rented accommodation. You do not need to have a formal written tenancy agreement to have tenancy rights, you have them until you give them up voluntarily or you are evicted through the legal process.

Firstly, your landlord must provide in writing an official notice to quit (NTQ), giving you a notice period to vacate the premises. It is worth checking if this notice is legitimate. A valid section 8 notice gives you a minimum of two weeks' notice, this is often 4 weeks in practice.

A valid section 21 must give you two months' notice. After this notice period the landlord must appeal to the court for an eviction order, which is then carried out by bailiffs. If this process is not followed, and in this order, it is an illegal eviction.

In terms of maintenance and repairs, these should be handled in a timely manner. There is some issue around landlord responsibility if damage is a result of student actions, horseplay, vandalism etc. But generally speaking, a landlord has the responsibility to ensure you have:

- A healthy, safe environment.
- Timely repairs and maintenance.
- A clean and pleasant living environment.

So, what constitutes a healthy safe environment? well everyone has their own expectations coming into rented accommodation and are some are willing to tolerate poor décor and older furniture, but the following issues would be considered unsafe:

- Unsafe, broken, walls, stairs, and roofs, if the outside can come in (i.e., rain/snow or wind), or something can fall and potentially cause harm.
- Broken or missing appliances: ovens, or fridges for example.
- Severe damp or mould issues (though students have a responsibility to clean bathrooms and kitchens during the tenancy period).
- Pests and rodents are sharing the flat (and not helping to pay the rent, the freeloaders).
- Improper sewage management.
- No adequate fire protection.

This list is not exhaustive, but hopefully gives you an idea of bad accommodation. Ideally you want to see your room or another like it in the same building prior to moving in. There should be no reason to move in or accept a flat in this condition.

However, if you sign a tenancy remotely and turn up to find it in an unsatisfactory condition, you could refuse to take up tenancy, seek legal advice and contact the local authorities, or if it is a small number of issues that needs resolving, ask your landlord to repair them as soon as possible.

If you are in a privately rented house and your landlord is refusing to carry out necessary works you would need to contact your institution asap, who can provide legal advice or contact the landlord and try to resolve the issue on your behalf. Contacting Citizens advice bureau or 'shelter' for advice are also wise options.

If you are in university managed accommodation or halls, the universities own maintenance team should be able to carry out necessary repairs.

For planned preventative maintenance they should warn you with 7 days' notice of their attendance and reason for attending (preferably by email). If they have given you this notice period, you cannot refuse them entry, although they would be limited to the areas and work described in the email. Students have a responsibility to check their student email account and keep lines of communication open.

For maintenance problems that arise during your tenancy you should report them through the university helpdesk or reporting process, the contact information should be readily available usually as a poster or on a noticeboard in your room or kitchen.

When you log a task for maintenance you are giving them permission to enter to carry out the repairs and they will not need to notify you of their attendance, although they will carry out works during reasonable hours, usually between 9-5 (office hours) to limit disruption.

Determining what is considered 'timely' repairs, would depend on the nature or severity of the issue. If you are without electricity, heating or are experiencing a flood in your room, this would be considered urgent, and an engineer will be called at any time of day or night.

Given the urgency, they may not inform you or your flat mates of their arrival, although an unannounced visit is the least of your concerns at that point.

Due to the nature of large electrical boards, boilers and so on, it may be that the issues cannot be resolved straight away, but they will be made safe. A leak/flood can be stopped by turning water off at the mains, and electrical systems can be isolated and made safe. In these cases, alternate options should be offered to you, if you are without central heating, temporary heaters should be offered, if you are without water in your ensuite, an appropriate alternate should be suggested. If they are not provided, ask for them.

Once the engineers have updated the housing management team and established a plan of action, they should contact you with an update to the repairs, and a due date for completion.

For any repair, large or small, the maintenance team will operate a triage system and prioritise jobs based on seriousness. Whilst your leaking tap might be serious for you, the flood in the nearby flat must be dealt with first and you may need to be a little patient.

If serious issues are not resolved in the first day or two you should contact the housing management team to identify the reason why, for less urgent tasks like a squeaky door hinge you should expect completion within 7-10 working days.

If you are unhappy with the situation over your repairs, the first step would be to lodge a complaint with the housing team, who can investigate. If there has been a mix-up, error or they have failed to deal with your issue on time, you may be entitled to a small measure of compensation.

It is worth noting again that housing managers are not mind readers, if you do not report issues to them, they cannot resolve them. Any complaint and investigation will consider the date you reported the issue.

I have had in my own role, issues where students have waited weeks to report an issue, they have become frustrated with their problem and by the time they reported it, they left for home and then claimed it was the universities' fault for their stress and negative experience. Whilst mistakes can occur with delayed repairs, the student is responsible for reporting issues in the first instance.

Send reports via email to ensure you have proof (it will show time/date in your sent/outbox). If you call someone, or speak by phone, follow up with an email to confirm details.

Medical requirements:

If you are a student with a medical issue or disability, you have the right to have some reasonable adjustments made in your student accommodation. Whilst this may limit your options of where to stay, there should be options available.

At the institute where I work, they can only house first year students. If you are a student with a disability or a medical requirement you can stay the entire 3 years of your course. They accomplish this by reserving 5% of its managed rooms for use by students with medical conditions, this will differ by institute, however. Students would need to fill out a special medical form at the time of application and may need their family doctor to sign off on this form. All higher education institutes should also have a dedicated person/department in place to provide support for student disabilities and medical issues.

Some examples of reasonable adjustments for students with medical conditions can include:

- Flashing fire alarms.
- Wheelchair accessible rooms.
- Handrails.
- Lowered shelving, switches, and kitchen facilities.
- Personal fridges for medication or to prevent contamination from allergens.
- Carer's rooms.
- Push button door access.
- Blue badge car parking.

It is worth noting that you may have to apply separately for disabled parking, make sure to mention this at the time of application.

Most medical requirements room for students with mobility issues will usually be located on ground floors of student accommodation, to aid in emergency evacuation. If you are on a higher floor and the fire alarm goes off, do not panic, there are solutions.

Many newer buildings will have emergency use elevators in place, which can be used during a fire alarm, however if yours does not, there should be fire refuge areas. These should be made clear, by signage, posters etc, but if you have any doubt, check with the building manager or landlord who should speak to you regarding a PEEP anyway (personal emergency evacuation plan).

Often these refuges are in stairwell foyers, which are safe from fire for much longer time periods, once there, you would need to call security or emergency services, who can affect a rescue.

Fire assembly points:

The Regulatory Reform (fire safety) Order 2005 requires institutes and 'responsible' persons to take appropriate fire precautions to ensure the safety of all persons within the building.

Fire routes and emergency exits must be kept clear, and students should also adhere to this to ensure the safety of yourselves and others. Furthermore, your own bedroom doors will be considered part of the fire route, if your own rooms are messy and door is blocked you are blocking your own fire routes.

Your landlord or building manager will fail your inspections should this be the case.

To summarise institutes will have to follow the following rules:

- Emergency routes and exits must lead directly as possible to a place of safety.
- Emergency routes and exits must be indicated by correct signage.

- Emergency routes and exits must be provided with adequate lighting, even in the case of failure of normal lighting (emergency lights on their own battery power).

- Emergency doors must be easily openable in an emergency and open in the direction of escape. These cannot be sliding or revolving doors.

- There should be established assembly points, which will be indicated on signage, these assembly points should ideally be 50 feet from the building.

Universities should carry out drills early in your contract to ensure you know what to do and where to congregate in the event of an emergency.

Fire safety:

19% of all current students have a broken fire alarm, many do not realise until much later. Fire alarms and smoke detectors should be tested when you first move into your property. Any that are broken should be reported to your landlord or building manager and should be dealt with as a matter of urgency

Many halls use built in systems which are tested weekly, although on rare occasions one or two individual room alarms may be broken (this can happen due to faults, tampering or covering smoke heads), if during a scheduled alarm you notice any that are not working, please report them as soon as possible.

More than half of all fires in students' halls start in kitchens. 55% of all fire related deaths among

18–24-year-olds are due to misuse of appliances and handling of hot substances.

The causes of kitchen fires are as follows:

- Cooking appliances (50%).
- Misuse of appliances (36%).
- Kitchen/food related (27%).
- Textiles, upholstery, or furniture (26%).
- Faulty appliances, cables, or plugs (16%).
- Smoking (6%).

Please note these figures may be misleading at first but there is some crossover, for example a fire caused by an appliance may be because that appliance was misused or faulty.

In the last five years, smoking and candles have been the cause of 1500 injuries to 18–24-year-olds, therefore all naked flames are banned from rooms in many institutes, so no incense, oil burners or candles are allowed. Candles alone cause more than five fires a day on average in the UK.

Ensure you turn off all unused electrical items overnight, that you do not overload sockets and extension lead and do not daisy chain. Do not leave hot items such as irons and hair curlers unattended when in use, curlers left on beds when hot are a common fire risk.

When cooking in kitchens do not leave cooking unattended and turn all hobs/ovens off when finished. It is also important that ovens are cleaned regularly, as oil can ignite if allowed to build up causing a fire. Lining cooking trays and grills with tin foil that can be removed and disposed of can help, but nothing beats a good old fashioned clean.

<u>GDPR:</u>

The General Data Protection Regulation is an EU (European Union) law covering data protection and privacy. It addresses the processing and transfer of personal data.

It is a complex and lengthy regulation; in terms of students, it guarantees the university, or your landlords will not misuse or share your personal details or data.

For those of us who work in universities it means very strict rules, the most frequent issue we find is dealing with the parents of students. Whilst we want to help and would gladly speak to students' parents, we must first have written permission from the student, naming their parent/s or representative as someone we can discuss their details with. Without this permission we could not even admit that their son or daughter is a student at our institution.

This of course has some worrying issues, occasionally we would receive worried phone calls from a parent suggesting they have not heard from their child, or that they were concerned they would do something 'silly', and they worry for their mental health.

According to the strict reading of the rules, we could not even confirm their child was a student and tenant with us. We would of course carry out a wellbeing check as soon as possible and if safe, advise the student to phone home, but this response leaves the parent feeling cold. It is however the law.

If you suspect you may need your parent to help discuss your issues with the university, send an email early that can be attached to your file, giving permission for the university too speak with them.

Tenant responsibilities:

Most tenant responsibilities will be laid out in the tenancy agreement signed on arrival, there will be items you should not have (banned list), or things you cannot do in the room, such as smoking or possessing drugs.

I have said it before, but please read your tenancy agreement and understand your responsibilities, believe it or not, a staggering 28% of students do not!

In short, you, the tenant, accepts responsibility for the state of decoration, all equipment, furniture, fixtures, and any fittings in your room from the point you take 'ownership'. If any damage or unnecessary wear occurs during the tenancy, the tenant will be held financially liable. The Landlord or building manager will consider fair wear and tear through a process of asset management for these costs, however.

If you jump on and break a 10-year-old sofa, you would not be charged the value of a brand-new replacement, the sofas value would be depreciated based on the age and condition at the time.

For example, a replacement sofa may cost the institute £1000, but you may only be charged £200 for damaging it. You can ask for a breakdown of any charges you receive, however it would be preferable for all involved to not jump on and break furniture.

It is advisable that at the time of moving in you carry out a full inventory, documenting (with pictures) the standard of the room, so that you can hand it back in the same condition and challenge any charges (charges are rare without good reason).

Furthermore, and as a surprise to most students, if there are shared areas within flats, all tenants who share these areas are equally responsible for all furniture, fixtures, fittings, and decoration of those areas. If a flat mate damages your kitchen table for example, does not admit it and no-one knows who it was, it is likely the flat will be held collectively responsible for recharges.

When your tenancy ends you must leave the property in a clean and tidy condition and return the keys. Some institutes and many in the private sector will take a deposit which may be non-returnable if you do not return your room in the condition, you found it in.

Part Two:

A safer student experience.

Much is said of the many challenges that students face, from worries around budgeting, making new friends and balancing your university workload. One of the areas that does not get as much attention is student safety.

In this section I will discuss the safety aspect of the student experience, the good, the bad and the ugly. The intention is not to scare you, but to prepare you.

From how to resolve conflict with flat mates to how to tackle the confusing world of relationships, sex and even drugs, there is a lot of information and data covering these areas, but much of this is not well known. In this section I combine industry knowledge with my own experiences working in personal safety and self-defence to delve into these issues and look at ways to avoid trouble.

Managing conflict.

Conflict is normal, whether between work colleagues, friends, or flat mates, it will happen, and we cannot expect two unique individuals to always agree on everything.

It could be that flat mates do not follow pre-established flat rules, it could be the result of miscommunication or a misunderstanding. It could also be due to differences of opinion about politics, cultures, or values.

Some of the annoying things housemates do can include, but not limited to:

- Leaving dirty dishes out.
- Not cleaning.
- Being too loud.
- Leaving food to go bad.
- Leaving lights or appliances on.
- Not removing hair from plug holes.
- Stealing food.
- Not changing toilet roll.
- Leaving windows open/heating.
- Leaving toilet seat up.
- Moving partners in.

The key to conflict management is not to fear or avoid conflict but learning how to resolve it in a healthy and respectable way. This will help you to develop strong high trust relationships.

Conflict is more than just a disagreement; it triggers emotions and stress in us that will not go away until the conflict is resolved. Yet these emotional responses are in opposition to the calm, levelheadedness needed to resolve the conflict.

Our bias from previous experiences can mean we fear or avoid conflict, we expect disagreements to end badly and that can leave us feeling powerless.

If you encounter conflict with flat mates, try to maintain the following behaviours:

- Communicate: Flat meetings, either with individuals, or groups. Get to the heart of the issue, be honest and fair, but be willing to listen and understand other parties too, pay attention to the feelings being expressed.

- Empathize: Try to see the other persons viewpoint. When emotional, scared, or angry we tend to lose this ability, control your emotions.

- Be calm: Be non-defensive if a flat mate is telling you how they feel, react respectfully.

- Forgive: Do not give into anger and resentment, allow everyone to move past minor disagreements. Allow people to make changes and appreciate we all make mistakes.

- Be tolerant: You cannot always agree on everything but work out what hill you want to die on. Sure, it is annoying they do not wash up until the end of the day, but is that a deal breaker as a flat mate?

- Respect: Understand and tolerate the differences in values, cultures, and ideas between different individuals.

- Compromise: Try to find a middle ground that suits most people.

Whatever happens do not tackle problems explosively head on with bad language and aggression, it is the responsibility of all of us to learn to deal amicably with people with whom we disagree.

If you cannot reconcile your differences speak with the halls management team. However, contacting authority figures before trying to resolve your issues informally may poison the relationship and escalate conflict within the flat.

There are three skills that can help with conflict resolution. The ability to control stress, emotional resilience, and effective communication

Stress management:

Stress interferes with your ability to communicate, hear, and empathise with what the other person is saying and reduces your ability to read body language, all key aspects of conflict resolution.

Keeping a stress journal can be important to identifying the sources of stress in your life. When you know where the stress is coming from you can start to accept responsibility for your part in creating or allowing it to happen. If you are constantly overworked, why would you then take on more work, this choice will lead you to being more overworked and more stressed.

Many people recommend the 4As approach to stress management:

Avoid: Take control of your environment. Is your bus getting caught in traffic regularly? Leave for class slightly earlier to avoid rush hour or try an alternate route or method (cycle). Do you wait too long at the cafeteria for lunch? why not pack your own lunch instead.

Stay clear of people who bother you: If you have a flat mate who annoys you, stay away from them, eat your meals at differing times to limit the time spent together.

Learn to say no: We all have limited time and energy and a constant stream of responsibilities and demands, we all like to be charitable, but taking on more than you have the time or energy for is foolish.

Alter: Ask others to change their behaviour. A respectful conversation may solve your problems, but you too have to be willing to change for others. Identify small problems and resolve them before they become bigger problems. Use 'I' statements instead of 'You', as in "I feel that I am the only one following the cleaning rota"

Manage your time more efficiently. Group together similar tasks, if you have multiple phone calls to make, do them together. Multiple off campus errands? Do them in one go and save making multiple trips. If you are concerned with a chatty member of the study group, mention in advance you have limited time and need to get topic 1 covered in that time.

Accept: Talk with friends. Getting things off your chest will not necessarily change anything, but venting will make you feel better. Having close friends and family to talk about problems with is amazing, be willing to offer an ear to your friends too.

Be willing to forgive. Do not let small issues drag you down, learn how to shrug and move on.

Learn from mistakes. You cannot change what has happened, but you can learn from it and prevent the same happening again.

Adapt: Adjust your expectations and standards. You need to clean your room, but is once a day too often? can you save time and energy doing it once a week instead

Reframe your situation. Your friends have cancelled on you, instead of getting down, consider it an opportunity to finish your module and do some laundry.

Look at the big picture: Will this issue matter to me in five years' time?

Adopt a mantra. Tell yourself "I can do this" and repeat it in tough situations.

Emotional resilience:

Emotional resilience is the ability to adapt to stressful situations, this is a tough skill to master, it requires a lot of self-reflection, many people will hide from their own strong emotions of anger, fear, and sadness. We are not honest with, or about ourselves.

The key to tackling complicated emotional issues, however, is to understand them in ourselves first. Having awareness of our emotions helps us to understand ourselves and our needs but also increases feelings of empathy for others.

Think back to arguments you have had in the past, did you handle the situation 100% the right way, did you dig your heels in too stubbornly, or say the wrong thing? Learn from your mistakes to become more resilient in future.

Effective communication:

Nonverbal communication is very important in conflict resolution. People rarely use the 'correct' words to convey their thoughts and feelings, especially when emotional. Being able to read body language and tone of voice will tell you much more than the words they speak.

Researchers from the 1960s found that our words only make up around 7% of our communication, 38% tone of voice and 55% nonverbal body language. Whilst this research has been challenged recently, the overall trend is true in practice, body language is very important.

Examples of body language are:

- Facial expressions.
- Gestures.
- Posture.
- Head movement.
- Eye contact.

Body language is universal to all people, for most it is subconscious, but others can use it consciously to express themselves. Think about a good public speaker, how they work a room, gesture to empathise their points, move around, and make eye contact to connect with the audience.

There is always a risk that no matter how well you manage conflict, the person you are dealing with actively wants to argue. Where resolution is impossible the only choice left is to walk away and seek help to resolve your issues.

If you ever require the involvement of a housing manager to resolve an issue between yourself and your flat mate, you must accept that you may not get the outcome you want, you may be forced to compromise.

I personally find this one of the hardest issues to manage among students, whilst as an external observer I can be more objective, I find emotions can run too high as each party tries to convince me of their side of the story. It can take me time to work out who is telling me the truth (people lie to me all the time).

If for safeguarding purposes I must separate the flat mates, we will tend to move the minimum number of people. So, if one housemate is feeling victimised by two others within the flat, I would move the one person as one empty room is easier to locate than two.

For many people in this position, this feels unfair, they are being bullied, and now being asked to move, people are very stubborn when they feel they are being unfairly treated.

For other managers and I, it is not about fairness, it is about safety, we must prevent an escalation of conflict, and I will deal with the tenancy breaches of those responsible immediately after I have addressed the safeguarding concerns.

I advocate that people work on emotional self-defence: that is to set healthier relationship standards in your life. Setting expectations will cause some people to take it personally, that is their issue not yours. It is a boundary not a grudge.

You need to establish certain rules around what behaviour is acceptable and what is not, therefore I suggest meeting with flat mates early and establishing those boundaries. There is a caveat however, the rules you establish must be reasonable and fair, you need to consider your own emotional wellbeing, but you cannot encroach on the feelings of others so that you can be coddled, there must be room for compromise.

Whilst you absolutely should expect flat mates to not be sexually explicit towards you (sexual harassment), you could not ban all general relationship talk within shared areas as this would not be fair on others who want to discuss their dates and partners with their flat mates. (Although in this extreme example I am sure some of the more explicit details may cross your boundaries which is why you need to have fair/balanced rules).

If you say something offensive on purpose to cause offense, that is on you, you are in the wrong. However, if you say something you know to be true and it causes offence, how other people react is down to them.

Sex.

In this chapter I want to discuss the more personal issue of sex, in terms of relationships, pitfalls and unfortunately sexual assaults.

Thankfully, most students will not experience sexual assault and have a peaceful enjoyable university life, however it is a real issue that does affect people, and something we should all know more about.

Assaults:

In 2020 the ONS reports that there were 162,936 sexual offences in England and Wales. The definitions of sexual assaults do vary and in my opinion are significant.

The crown prosecution service (CPS) regards a range of crimes to be a sexual offence including:

- Domestic abuse.
- Rape.
- Stalking.
- Harassment.
- Honour based violence.
- Forced marriage.
- Female genital mutilation.
- Child abuse.
- Human trafficking for sexual exploitation.
- Prostitution.
- Pornography (including revenge porn and making indecent images of children)

- Obscenity.

Whereas other independent organisations spread the net wider and will include catcalling and unwanted flirting as harassment.

Since I will be using official government figures I am assuming the list above is an accurate definition.

When dealing with cases of rape it is important to understand that the legal definition prevents a woman from carrying out a rape. Any attacks by women, either on men or other women would be listed as a sexual assault rather than rape.

This is because rape is defined as the penetration of the vagina, anus, or mouth by the penis without consent. As a result, any data that describes rape will almost exclusively list men as the perpetrators.

Sexual assault is defined as one person intentionally touching another sexually without their consent.

The 2020 crime survey showed 1.6 million adults aged 16-74 had experienced sexual assault by rape, this is 3.8% of the UK population, of this number:

- 49% had been the victim of a previous attack.
- 44% were victimized by partner or ex-partner.
- 37% were assaulted by someone they know.
- 9% were assaulted in public.
- 37% were assaulted in their home.
- 54% said physical force was used.
- Only 16% reported the assault

In total 7.1% of UK women over 16 have experienced rape or experienced attempted rape compared to 0.5% for UK men. Almost all assaults are carried out by males (98%) most attackers were of a similar age to their victims.

Where men were the victim, its far more likely that their attacker was a stranger (43%) than is the case for women (15%) who are more likely to be attacked by someone they know.

Worryingly and somewhat telling 49% of rape victims were under the influence of alcohol at the time of their attack.

The fallout from rapes, or other sexual assault can be devastating, most victims will report ongoing mental or emotional problems, specifically 47% of male victims and 63% of female victims. 12% of men and 10% of women who are victims of these assaults later try to commit suicide.

Despite only 16% of cases being reported, in 21% of investigated cases the perpetrator was charged. Some organisations say that only 1 in every 100 victims get justice, whilst this is hard to quantify and does not seem to be supported by evidence, the lack of reporting is a concern. To tackle this the CPS has a special team of prosecutors across England and Wales who are trained to deal with cases involving allegations of a sexual nature.

Special measures were introduced in 2006 via the 'Code of practice for victims of crime' and can be applied during court proceedings.
These can include:

- Screens to shield witnesses.
- Live video link to give evidence from a separate and safer room.
- Allow witnesses to give evidence in private.

- Allow witnesses to give evidence in a video-recorded interview.

Consent:

Consent is a key issue for people to consider in all instances where sexual contact occurs. The Sexual offences act 2003 defines consent as: engaging in sexual activity if they agree by choice and they have the freedom and capacity to make that choice.

Consent can be given but with limitations, for example a person may consent to vaginal penetration but not anal penetration. Further conditions may also apply, such as the use of a condom.

At any point during sexual activity consent can be withdrawn, failure to stop when asked would be considered an assault or rape.

Consent has two major factors: Free choice and capacity. Free choice is unlikely to be given in instances where people are threatened, blackmailed, or coerced. Capacity usually refers to whether the individuals were under the influence of drugs or alcohol, although may also include mental fitness.

The issue of alcohol and sex can be a minefield to navigate and if I am completely honest, I do not know where the lines are precisely drawn from a legal perspective. What is clear though, is that some people do operate in bad faith, they will push alcohol on their partner, in the hopes that once intoxicated they will "consent" to sex, this is no different than using a date rape drug.

If your partner is slurring words, stumbling around, acting incoherently, or passed out, they do not have the capacity to consent, and any sexual contact is likely to be considered an assault.

The part here that seems unfair to young men is that almost no men who get drunk and have sex are likely to report it as an assault, whereas some women do. The only solution is to ensure you were operating within the boundaries of the law.

To stay safe, efforts must be established to obtain consent before sexual activity can take place. Remember silence is not consent and people who are impaired do not have the capacity to give consent.

An old anti-drinking campaign poster that I saw around my current institution implied that if both people were drunk the man would be guilty of rape. Even if he himself was drunk too? that seems very one sided and hard to quantify. If both were drunk, why are we only blaming the man? This is not something we should gloss over, it clearly is a concern as false allegations can ruin a person's life, and unfortunately false allegations tend to impact men far more than women.

On the flip side however, far more women are victims of rape and assault than men, and many either do not report it for fear of not being believed, or do not get justice as proving an assault is extremely difficult.

Ideally matters of guilt or innocence would be handled in the courtroom, however as mentioned there is no legal standard on how intoxicated is too intoxicated to give consent. There is no objective consensus in the public square either, ask a dozen people, you will get many different answers. "One drink", "two drinks". "Sober or not at all" and the more extreme "if they are conscious and don't say stop".

To comment on the campaign poster considering the law as written, a female could report that she was assaulted whilst drunk, the man who had sex with her could not use consent as an excuse during the case because she had no capacity to give it. However due to his own intoxication he could claim that he was not able to realise she was too intoxicated and was acting in good faith with perceived consent. He potentially could also counter claim that he too was too intoxicated to give consent.

The problem with the latter is that it is mutually assured destruction and not a defence to the allegations made against him. To be fair, these issues are hard to prosecute, I suspect few are successfully prosecuted which may have an impact on overall figures (keeping them low). Furthermore, there is an additional element of unfairness, as men tend to get much higher sentences for 'rape' than women get for sexual assaults.

Rape carries a sentencing range of between 4-19 years, dependant on the harm caused.

Category A: A rape that involves, abduction, violence or the victim is vulnerable (handicapped etc) sentencing starts at 15 years (range of 13-19 years).

Category B: Rape with no prior motivation or violence, victim became pregnant or infected with STIs. Sentencing starts at 8 years (range of 7-9 years).

Category C: No aggravating harm factors, more applicable to drunk sex. Sentencing starts at 5 years (range of 4-7 years).

Sentencing start points will be measured against aggravating or mitigating factors to give a sentence within the range noted.

For sexual assault, the sentencing range is between 26 weeks and 4 years for the most heinous acts.

A man can coerce a drunk woman into penetrative sex and be imprisoned for 5 years for rape, a woman can coerce a drunk man into penetrative sex and may not even see the inside of a prison cell (suspended sentence) or sentenced to 26 weeks. Quite the disparity.

Allegations of sexual assault could lead to additional problems, at this point you are still considered innocent (until proven guilty), however due to safeguarding measures you may be asked to move from your room or your halls. You may also be asked to study online until the issue is resolved. It can lead to suspensions and expulsions even without a criminal conviction.

If Police investigate the complaint, institutes will have to cease their own investigations and await the outcome of the criminal case. Police investigations can take months to complete, leaving you in limbo, unsure if you will lose your university place or even be prosecuted.

If the worst happens and you are raped or sexually assaulted (or have been previously). It is important to know that it was not your fault, and you absolutely should get help.

Firstly, you should seek medical help, there may be a risk of pregnancy or STIs and if you later want the crime to be investigated, getting forensic evidence will help your case.

If you wish to report your assault, call the police as soon as possible, try not to shower/wash, or change clothes as this may destroy key forensic evidence.

The NHS operates Sexual assault referral centres that are open 24 hours a day. You can search the nearest location online or at the following web address: **https://www.nhs.uk/service-search/other-services/Rape-and-sexual-assault-referral-centres/LocationSearch/364**. Your institute may also have an independent sexual violence Liaison who you could contact.

Alternatively, there are many organisations that can offer support such as:

- Rape crisis: 0808 802 9999
- Victim support: 0808 168 9111
- The survivor's trust: 01788 550554
- Male survivor's partnership: 0808 800 5005

Before moving on from this subject I want to revisit the subject of consent. I do know of a case where a male and female had consensual sex, but in the days following, the female decided that due to her unstable mental health (which the male was not aware of), she was not sure she was in the right 'head space' to give consent at the time and had regrets.

Whilst we can have empathy with the young lady involved, mental health is not something to take lightly, we cannot accept with withdrawal of consent after the fact, it is just not fair to the young man in this case. Both parties had consented to the act, and did not remove consent during, and there was no coercion or alcohol involved.

Whilst this will sound harsh, it is the responsibility of every individual to accept the consequences of their actions, if you are not in a good 'head space', do not consent to or engage in something which you may later regret.

As a side note to this, I fully accept there may be incidents where one person can take advantage of an individual suffering mental health issues for their own sexual gratification, for the sake of the argument above I consider this coercion and assault, as would many in the legal system.

Spiking:

There has been a dramatic increase in spiking over the past few years, especially concerning students. This is where people put drugs into your drink, usually for the purposes of carrying out sexual assaults (date rape), but not always. It can be common for people to give you strong alcohol to get you drunk quicker, this is also considered spiking. This could be as simple as asking for a single vodka and coke and your friend gets you a double to 'loosen you up'.

Drinking, like sex should involve consent, by giving people more alcohol than they ask for, the person cannot monitor their consumption correctly.

It has been reported that 12.6% of the public, specifically 15% of Women and 7% of men have been spiked at some point with alcohol or drugs. A separate survey of students showed that 11% have been spiked. Of these only 8% of people report it and more worryingly 35% of all spiking occurs at private parties.

To avoid having your drink spiked, consider the following:

- Always buy your own drinks and watch it being poured.
- Do not accept drinks from strangers.
- Never leave your drink unattended.
- Do not drink or taste anyone else's drink.
- If in doubt throw away your drink, if you think it tastes odd or looks like it has been mixed with something throw it out.
- Do not drink to excess, you are more likely to be caught out and not paying attention if intoxicated.

The second method of spiking is 'needle spiking', injecting drugs such as Rohypnol or Gamma Hydroxybutyrate (GHB), so called date rape drugs.

Needle spiking is a strange issue, since slipping something into a drink is far easier than trying to stick a needle into someone, but with people being more aware with their drinks, the attackers have evolved.

There is some debate on whether it is feasible for someone to be injected without noticing, but once you are intoxicated, it is possible you may not be aware.

Clearly there have been individual cases with strong evidence of injection but researchers from the global drugs survey believe that given the difficulty of needle spiking we should be far more worried about drink spiking.

If you think you have been spiked, if you start to feel strange, sick, or drunk when you know you should not be (only had the one). You need to seek help immediately:

- If possible, contact a friend, have them take you home if they are with you, or pick you up.

- Seek help from the venue staff and management.
- If you become unwell, seek medical help.

If you have any doubts, concerns or are otherwise being harassed or feel unsafe whilst in a pub or club, go to a member of staff and ask for help, in some areas you can ask to see "Angela". The ask for Angela campaign started in Lincolnshire and has become popular in many establishments across the UK and wider world. It is a code word that informs the staff you are in distress and need of assistance.

It would be wise to contact local pubs and bars to see if they run this system or another similar one before going out for the night. Learn the safety words and plan to stay safe.

Universities:

Sexual assaults reported at UK universities have doubled in the four years leading up to 2019 (112% increase). In 2019 there were 500 cases on UK campuses alone.

Increases in assaults are in part due to new anonymous reporting tools at most universities, meaning more people feel comfortable making complaints without fear of reprisal. Whilst many still do not want to report, we are seeing a large increase in people coming forward to report their assaults.

One study shows 1 in 5 women are assaulted during their time at university. But does not specify a definition of sexual assault. Some, for example, suggested unwanted remarks (catcalling) or unwanted advances/flirting to be an assault.

With ONS showing 1 in 5 women experiencing assault during their lifetime I would challenge the study that 1 in 5 are assaulted in university, but it is irrelevant to have that debate here, as every assault is one too many. What is clear from the stats, however, is that most victims of sexual assault will know their attackers, and it will likely be a partner or former partner.

Most universities have a dedicated wellbeing team and sexual violence liaison officer. There are many ways to report an assault and the institutes will support you throughout, there is always help available. Safeguarding methods will be taken, even if you choose not to press charges, this could mean moving you to a safer area or moving the other person away from you.

Social justice:

Whilst there has been much needed emphasis on the experiences of young people, specifically women in society and at university, not all social justice campaigns send the right message or achieve the intended outcomes.

Take the "me-too" movement for example. Studies documenting this movement, initially showed that 63% of women had experienced harassment in the workplace, a frightening figure.

As a result of the Me-too movement, it was reported that 74% of women were now more comfortable speaking out against harassment and 77% of men are more conscious of potentially inappropriate behaviour, a good result.

However, further studies show that because of 'me-too' around 20% of both men and women are now less willing to hire attractive women, 22% of men and 44% of women are now less likely to involve female colleagues in social interactions, such as after work drinks. In addition, 33% of men are now reluctant to have a one-on-one meeting with a female colleague.

Attitudes have changed slightly, but most women still think men will continue to harass them but take more care to not get caught, whilst most men have fears of being unfairly accused of harassment. What was meant to highlight and tackle a serious social issue has had disastrous effects on inter gender work relations.

The harsh reality is that whilst some guilty parties were held to account (Bill Cosby et al), in other instances the idea that we should 'believe all women' has resulted in some innocent men being harmed by false accusations. Some have lost their careers, others have lost families or university places, some have taken their own lives as a result.

It is a hard road to walk, we want to hold the guilty accountable, but we need to protect the innocent from having their lives destroyed. Merely believing all women is not appropriate, since some women are bad faith actors, they lie, cheat, and steal just like some men do.

I am honestly not sure where we go from here as a society, but as individuals, we must all take responsibility for our own safety and ignore ideology. We must deal with what is, not what should be, we need to be practical. Or as Johnathon Haidt says in his book 'Coddling of the American mind', we need to "Prepare the child for the road, not the road for the child"

When marching for women's rights and safety, we should think about this:
Those men who agree with you, do not need to be told. Those men that need to be told, will not listen to you. This is not to say that social action is not useful or important to create societal change (it is), but we should refrain from blaming all men for the actions of a minority and avoid the destruction of innocent lives in a quest for justice.

Attitudes:

Attitudes towards sex have changed much over the last few decades. An academic paper from America studied the changes in sexual behaviour and attitudes between 1972 and 2012. In this period the following trends have appeared:

- Acceptance of premarital sex increased from 29% to 58%.

- Acceptance of same sex activity increased from 20% to 58%. (People are far more accepting of female same sex than male).

- Early teens who engage in sex (14-16 years old) increased from 4% to 6%.

This is similar for other western countries, with the second Australian study of health and relationships and the UK national surveys of sexual attitudes and lifestyles, showing the same trends.

In the UK, this could be argued that we have developed very liberal attitudes to sex, but there are some trends that show the opposite. Rates of extra marital sex, Polygamy, and sex with multiple partners (at the same time) have decreased over this time.

The one statistic that interests me is the attitudes towards one-night stands, in 1990 around half of all people aged 16 to 44 viewed one night stands as wrong, this fell to around 20% in 2010, although it seems to have levelled off at that rate.

For those who find one-night stands are inappropriate, they may feel shame if something happens, usually under the influence, as alcohol reduces inhibitions. Shame is just our natural response to crossing our own boundaries. Understanding ourselves and our own values is key to setting healthy boundaries, shame is just an unconscious reminder of where those boundaries are.

There are now very different priorities than when my parents were teens (late 70s, early 80's), back then people were married in their 20s hoping to buy a home and starting a family. For example, the UK currently has the lowest rates of marriage since records began in 1862, rates have been steadily dropping since 1970 largely due to:

- Higher divorce rates, young people seeing the impact from parents separating.
- Cost of marriage.
- Relaxed attitudes towards co-habiting and pre-marital sex.

In addition, there are more people in higher education than ever before, they tend to wait to get married, work on careers and push back having children until their mid to late 30s, and have fewer children overall (if at all).

Studies show that those who marry having had fewer previous sexual partners (or none) tend to have the lowest divorce rates. There does seem to be a complex yet visible relationship between the number of previous sexual partners and marital happiness. The more partners you have before settling down can make you unhappier in your marriage.

There was a concern that the changing attitudes towards one-night stands would increase the availability of cheap sex and thus men would not commit to marriage. Whilst rates of marriage have decreased, we have not seen the increase in sexual activity among men this predicted, Millennials have had fewer sex partners on average than the previous generation.

General trends:

- Men have more sexual partners on average than women.
- There is little difference between women in Higher education and those not in higher education in numbers of sexual partners.
- Number of sexual partners for men in higher education is noticeably less than those not in higher education.
- 90% of women have under 10 partners in their lives, 90% of men have less than 30.
- By age 44 the average man has had 7 partners, the average woman 4.

Having more sexual partners than the average increases your sexual health risks, from STIs but also for your mental health. Promiscuous behaviours are linked to risk taking, this can lead to issues with self-image, unable to create relationships and even depression. These issues themselves can cause people to become more promiscuous creating a negative feedback loop.

Even though many of you are still young and exploring life, do ask the question of what you want from life, do you want a healthy marriage and children later? Maybe the answer to this question could shape your current day decision making for a healthier outcome.

Studies show that long term relationships improve emotion, physical and sexual health.

Couples in long term relationships are also less likely to suffer from domestic violence.

There is an idea that because sex makes you happy, and more sex makes you 'more' happy, that promiscuity is good for your 'happiness', one study even shows that for women sex makes them happier than any other activity. However, studies also show that promiscuity creates the opposite: People with fewer sexual partners tend to be happier.

The abridged version: Having multiple sexual partners is not good for your happiness, mental health, and sexual health. It is more likely to result in unhappy marriages in the future. A healthy sex life is good for you but should be kept within fewer, longer-term relationships.

Online dating:

Dating apps, make meeting people effortless, it is something you can do from the comfort and safety of your room. The apps use questions to match you with like-minded people, all you need to do is 'swipe right'.

Data sharing is a huge concern, dating sites keep your personal information even if you were to delete your account and any information you share with 'dates' can be used against you by scammers, blackmailers, or predators.

Scammers: Create false profiles to earn your trust, create a relationship and then try and coerce you into paying for a medical or travel emergency which they promise to pay back (but never do).

Predators: Will seek out vulnerable people based on details from their profiles, those with mental health issues, younger more naïve people. It has also been known for sexual predators to seek out relationships with single mothers hoping to gain access to their children.

However, online dating is very superficial, concentrating on looks and profile pictures that are usually airbrushed and people will commonly misrepresent themselves in a myriad of other ways too. It also breeds a 'shopper mentality': with so many choices available there is no need to commit to relationships, you can jump from one person to the next, looking for easy one-night stands with no strings attached, creating a transactional experience.

There is no substitute for meeting people in the real world, learning how to talk to them and getting to know the real person, not some made up profile.

Going on dates:

If you do decide to try online dating, you need to manage your expectations. Do not consider the chats you have as leading to relationships or sex, you are just getting to know people. This will take the pressure and anxiety off your shoulders, and you can concentrate on just having great conversations. Eventually you will speak with someone who you find interesting enough to meet, but you need to be patient.

You do have to be open and honest with people, and this is equally true of any dating scenario, you need to let people get to know the real you and you need to know the real 'them'. This can be a real leap of faith, but it will also help you to discover more about yourself too.

In terms of managing expectations, remove any thought of meeting 'the one', the 'perfect match'. Everyone will have differences and even the closest people will not agree on everything.

I realise that 18-year-olds probably do not want dating advice from an 'oldie' who has been married since before they were born, but I would like to include some tips on the dating experience regardless. Keep it about the conversation, going to a cinema is a nice easy, sometimes cheap date (especially if you get student ticket deals), but you do not learn much about each other apart from what flavour popcorn you both prefer. You want to be in a setting that promotes talk, ask open questions, and listen to them.

Try and carry out an activity together, go for a walk together or visit a museum or gallery, have lunch in the park, be casual.

Most importantly you do not have to meet people online, universities have a diverse range of people with differing interests and personalities. Join societies and groups and get chatting to like-minded people, you do not need the formal dating structure to get to know people. Its more dynamic, good for your mental health and relationships will evolve naturally, some will become friends, others may become more.

Finally do not try too hard, nobody likes desperation!

Pornography:

With phones in the hands of today's youth, the internet is only a few keystrokes away. With teenage sexual curiosity in the driving seat, it is common to explore for material that will indulge their desires.

The idea behind pornography is not inherently dangerous, although there is much to be concerned about in the industries that create that material. It is natural for teenagers to explore their sexuality alongside masturbation to work out what they like, what they do not and to learn more about sexual acts. The danger however is that, as it is the source of primary sexual education for young men (who are the majority of consumers), the effect pornography has on their expectations and behaviours is highly damaging.

Research has shown that among higher education men, the majority (51%) watch pornography several times a week, with 13.5% watching it daily. More worryingly this research has shown for many of these young men, they use previously viewed images to maintain arousal during sex and some even prefer pornography to the real thing.

There seems to be a correlation between what happens in pornographic material and the attitudes of young men towards sex, including behaviours that lead to sexual violence, control, degradation, and hostility towards female partners. It changes attitudes towards an increase in unsafe sex, choking/strangulation and domination and has been proven through studies to increase sexist attitudes towards women who are expected to be submissive.

Studies have shown that 88% of available pornography shows aggression or dominance towards women, and that more effort should be made to create and view ethical pornography instead.

Sex work among students:

Recent studies show that 4-5% of undergraduate students engage in sex work during their time at university, 7% of students turned to sex or adult work during the pandemic as businesses closed and their income dried up (77% of these students are female). The most popular types of 'sex work' can include selling nude photos (over snapchat or other social media), selling used underwear, phone sex and offering live chat and webcam services.

Only 7% of sex workers turn to prostitution. There has however been a large rise in sugar dating: Predominately female students exchanging companionship and sex for financial support from older men. Sugar dating site SeekingArrangement.com has 400,000 UK members of which 40% are students, this trend rose exponentially since 2012 when university fees jumped to £9000 per year, showing a clear correlation between financial hardship and student sex work.

Sugar dating gets around prostitution laws by claiming the money is for 'companionship' only.

Whilst this may seem like an easy way to pay the bills, psychologists warn about the impact of sex work on mental health: Due to the stigma attached to sex work, the workers may not feel comfortable talking about dangerous or vulnerable experiences. They feel isolated and alone. Repeated experiences can lead to anxiety and emotional distress.

It is important to know that there are hardship funds and support available for struggling students, there is no need to enter a potentially dangerous and degrading transactional situation to make ends meet. Contact your university to enquire about hardship funds, additionally if you are a care leaver, or from a low-income background you may be able to claim extra funds to help you through.

Sexual transmitted infections:

There are more than 25 different STIs that can be spread during sexual contact. Worldwide it is estimated that one million people contract an STI every day, most people who have them have no symptoms and can easily pass them on without knowing. Around half of all new cases are in the 15-24 age group despite them making up on a small minority of sexually active people.

If left untreated STIs can cause severe health issues such as cervical cancer, infertility, and problems during pregnancy later in life. It is an issue which has greater health consequences for women than men.

Most STIs, but not all, can be successfully treated, some however can have lasting impacts on your life, such as HIV.

Young women seem very susceptible to STIs, this is due to cells lining the cervix at younger ages that are more prone to infection, therefore sexually active young women should get STI screenings and regular smear checks (tests start at 25 in the UK).

The rates of STIs have risen over past years, the lessons learned by my generation have been forgotten in recent years (by all age groups). Overall trends include:

- 26% rise in gonorrhoea.
- 10% rise in syphilis.
- Gay and bisexual men have seen an 83% jump in rates of chlamydia.
- 65 and overs have seen a 23% increase in STIs since 2014
- 45-64 age group have seen an increase of 18% in men and 4% in women.

The most common STIs include the following (in alphabetical order):

Chancroid: Caused by a bacterium, spreads by vaginal or anal sex or skin contact with sores. Symptoms include genital sores, vaginal discharge, a burning feeling when urinating and swollen lymph nodes in the groin. Can be treated with antibiotics.
Chlamydia: Caused by a bacterium that exists within semen and vaginal secretions, spreads by vaginal, anal, or oral sex when not using a barrier

contraceptive (condom). Can also be passed from pregnant mothers to infants during childbirth.

Symptoms include vaginal discharge and burning during urination, but most people are asymptomatic. If not treated can lead to infertility.

Can be treated with antibiotics.

Genital Warts: Caused by a virus (HPV – human papillomavirus), causes warts on the genitals that can lead to cancer, spreads through skin to skin contact during oral, vaginal, or anal sex. Due to skin-to-skin transmission, condoms do not prevent transmission. Whilst it cannot be cured, HPV vaccinations are available to young teenagers, which should be taken prior to engaging in sexual contact.

Gonorrhoea (the clap): Caused by a bacterium that exists within semen and vaginal secretions, spreads by vaginal, anal, or oral sex when not using a barrier contraceptive. Symptoms include a yellow/greenish vaginal discharge and burning feeling when urinating, can also affect the anus and throat. Many people are asymptomatic. If untreated may cause permanent infertility. It can be treated with antibiotics.

Herpes: Caused by a virus that lives in the nerves. There are two types, HSV-1 causes cold sores around the mouth, HSV-2 causes sores in the genital area. It spreads through skin-to-skin contact.

Symptoms include painful and itchy blisters that come and go through 'outbreaks.' HSV-2 is more common for women, and it can be spread to infants during pregnancy. There is no cure for Herpes, it can only be managed with medication.

HIV: Human immunodeficiency virus, is the virus that causes AIDs, it exists in blood, semen, vaginal secretions, and breast milk. It spreads through vaginal, anal or oral sex when not using a barrier contraceptive. If untreated HIV can lead to severe health issues and early death, although it cannot be cured, drugs can be used to control the 'viral load' which can keep you healthier for longer and greatly reduce the possibility of transmission.

Hepatitis: Caused by viruses that exist in blood, semen, vaginal secretions and breast milk, results in inflammation of the liver although some people are asymptomatic. There are two main forms, Hepatitis B (HBV) and Hepatitis C (HCV).
There is a vaccine that prevents HBV and HCV can be cured.

Lice (Crabs): Lice live in the pubic hair around the genitals and are transmitted by skin-to-skin contact, they can also spread via clothes and bedding. Symptoms include itching and visible eggs in pubic hair. Can be treated with over-the-counter medication, all clothes, bedding, and towels should be washed on a hot cycle to prevent reinfection and spreading.

Syphilis: Cause by a bacterium, spreads by vaginal, anal, or oral sex when not using a barrier contraceptive Symptoms vary as it has several 'phases', early symptoms can include painful open sores in the genital area (or mouth or anus), these sores usually heal within 3-6 weeks. The second phase symptoms can include a rash and hair loss. If left untreated the later stages can involve damage to the heart and brain. This can be passed to infants during pregnancy and childbirth. This Can be treated with antibiotics.

Trichomoniasis: Caused by a single celled germ called protozoa and causes vaginal infections, spreads by vaginal, anal, or oral sex when not using a barrier contraceptive. Symptoms include foamy, foul-smelling vaginal discharge and itching, although some people are asymptomatic. This Can be treated with antibiotics.

The risks of getting an STI can be mitigated by practicing safer sex:

- Use condoms (male) or Femidoms (female) for vaginal or anal sex. Many people who use the pill or other forms of birth control will not use condoms as the risk of pregnancy is mitigated, however the pill offers no protection against STIs.
- Use condoms without lubricant for oral sex. Most people do not, as there is no risk of pregnancy, but STI risks must be considered. Plastic barriers for oral sex on a woman can also be used.
- Do not use oil-based products with condoms as they can destroy the latex, these include Vaseline, coconut oil, vegetable oil or body lotion.
- Wash shared sex toys after use and do not share or reuse condoms.

When in a sexual relationship, do not assume you or your partner is clear of STIs, many people are asymptomatic and if either of you have had previous sexual partners you may be carrying an STI.

Condoms can be collected free of charge from most contraceptive clinics and some GP surgeries.

If you have any concerns about STIs, contact your family doctor to discuss screening.

Drugs.

Drugs can be defined as any substance which has a physiological or psychological effect when introduced into the body.

In 2020 there were 208,961 drug offences in England and Wales. In this same time there were 4561 deaths due to drug poisoning, two thirds of these because of drug misuse. These numbers do not include Scotland, which is considered the drug death capital of the world and has over twice the number of drug related deaths than any other European country. Across the UK, men are twice as likely to die from drug poisoning than women, this includes alcohol.

The joint NUS/release survey in 2018 (called taking the hit: student drug use and how institutions respond) shows that:

- 56% of all students have used drugs at some point in higher education.
- 62% of students have relaxed attitudes towards drug use, 84% of students do not feel pressure to take drugs.
- 86% of students who use drugs do so in university halls/rooms.

There are three main reasons for drug use:
- Recreational.
- To enhance social interaction.
- Help with stress.

Commonly used drugs by students include (in alphabetical order):

- Alcohol.
- Amphetamines.
- Benzodiazepines.
- Cannabis.
- Cocaine.
- Ecstasy.
- Ketamine.
- LSD.
- Nitrous oxide.
- Psilocybin.
- Study/smart drugs.

Alcohol:

UK has highest per capita alcohol consumption in the world, there are an estimated 1.6 million alcohol dependant people, with only around 18% getting treatment. Research shows the following:

- 24% of adults drink more than the recommended amounts.
- 27% binge drink (more than 8 units for men, 6 for women)
- In 2020 in England and Wales there were 7423 alcohol related deaths, a 19.6% increase on the previous year. Although we do know that lockdowns exacerbated existing issues around drinking.
- In 2019/20 in England there were 976,425 hospital admissions relating to alcohol.

- Alcohol is a causal factor in more than 60 medical conditions, including multiple cancers, high blood pressure, depression, and liver cirrhosis.
- Men are more than twice as likely to die from alcohol related issues than women.

Despite all the statistics, since 2005 the overall amount of alcohol consumed and the proportion of people who drink have all fallen, and this is more pronounced among younger people. Although 16–24-year-olds are the least likely group to drink, when individuals of this age do drink, they are more likely to drink to excess.

As previously mentioned, 49% of sexual assault victims were intoxicated by alcohol and alcohol is a factor in 30% of all suicides. Monitoring your alcohol intake and its effect on your mental health is key to your safety and wellbeing. Drinking because you are depressed. stressed or anxious is akin to pouring fuel on a fire.

We also must consider the impact of alcohol on aggression, especially amongst younger males, although something we increasingly see in younger females too. Not only does alcohol reduce your inhibitions, making you more likely to do things you would not normally do (ask out the girl, jump the fence into the river, steal my building signs – you know who you are!). It can cause something referred to as alcohol myopia, where we cannot think clearly and our attention is narrowed, we miss social cues and misinterpret situations and people's words. This can lead to anger and increase the levels of conflict and may end in violence.

In 39% of all violent attacks in 2018 the perpetrator was under the influence of alcohol and in 30% of partner abuse cases, alcohol was a factor.

If you are a habitual drinker, you often feel the need to drink you may need to seek advice and help. You may find your drinking gets you into trouble, you are late for plans and work, or other people may have warned you about your alcohol intake. Once you realise you have a problem, you must accept you are unlikely to control the issue without help and support, the first stop should be an honest conversation with your GP.

If you (or someone you know) becomes physically dependant on alcohol, going cold turkey can be harmful and lead to some nasty withdrawal symptoms that can include:

- Anxiety.
- Tremors.
- Sweating.
- Vomiting.
- Hallucinations.
- Seizures.

In this case there may need to be a managed reduction of alcohol or the use of medication to control withdrawal symptoms. Some useful helplines include:

- Drink line: 0300 123 1110
- Alcoholics Anonymous (AA): 0800 9177 650

There are some common 'symptoms' of alcohol abuse in others, these can include:

- Making excuses to drink, such as stress, the need to relax etc.
- Mood swings.
- Choosing to drink over other responsibilities.
- Drinking alone.
- Becoming distant from friends and family.

It can be hard to talk to someone else about their drinking habits, if you decide to do so, think about what you will say in advance, but think about being as calm and positive as possible as being confrontational will make the situation worse. Wait for the perfect moment, ideally when they are not intoxicated and when they are alert and actively engaging with you. It is very important to start slowly, keep the conversation short and consider it the start of a longer conversation to be had later. You should aim for smaller sentences with simple language, start sentences with 'I' as in "I am concerned about you" rather than 'you, as in "you have a problem".

Be patient with them, allow them time to think and respond to what you are saying, but be ready for a negative reaction. Anger is common, but it is likely they are not actually angry, but feeling threatened. If it gets too heated end the conversation but leave it open to pick up another day. Say something along the lines of "ok let's put a pin in this for now, but can we talk some more tomorrow?".

Whilst you are trying to help someone else, you may find your own wellbeing may be affected. Remember to seek help if you need it, there is plenty of support available both via your institution and independent organisations and charities.

It is common that a person can have multiple addictions at once or mix alcohol with other drugs to experiment towards a greater high. Alcohol is a natural depressant and if combined with other 'depressant' drugs such as opioids, heroin, marijuana, or cocaine can produce extreme effects in the body. Short term effects can include confusion and poor cognitive function, respiratory depression, elevated heart rates, seizures and in the worst cases it can be fatal.

In this next section I will discuss the drugs commonly available to students in higher education, their effects on people and the dangers of taking them. In alphabetical order:

Amphetamines:

The term Amphetamines refers to a class of drug that stimulates the central nervous system, acting on the serotonin and dopamine levels to give a feel-good sensation. Studies suggest it is the third most abused drug in the UK behind alcohol and cannabis. Prescribed versions of these drugs can improve cognition, focus and alertness. One example is Adderall which is commonly prescribed to treat attention deficit hyperactivity disorder (ADHD) and narcolepsy.

Often referred to as speed or uppers, many students treat these drugs as a form of study drug, which will be covered in more depth in their own section. However, when used in this way Amphetamines often fail to live up to expectations, this is because they alter the brain chemistry and impair the brains' ability to change and learn as it processes information. Despite their intentions students who use regularly can find themselves unable to focus when studying under the influence of these drugs and may soon end up dependant on them by needing to take more each time.

Amphetamines can negatively affect moods and sleep patterns which can harm cognitive function, they can also increase feelings of stress, anxiety, depression, irritability and even psychosis. It can lead to rapid weight loss, heart failure, impotence, and can trigger suicidal tendencies. A terrible combination with an already high-risk group for mental health concerns.

Whilst I would not recommend taking this drug, if you are taking it, you should not exceed 60mg, as at this dosage the drug can have severe impacts on your physical and mental health.

Benzodiazepines:

Commonly called Benzos, these are a type of sedative that depress the central nervous system. They are commonly used to treat anxiety (diazepam is commonly prescribed for this), night terrors, obsessive compulsive disorder (OCD) and some minor personality disorders.

This drug works by increasing the effects of a naturally occurring brain chemical called gamma aminobutyric acid (GABA). This chemical reduces activity in areas of the brain associated with:

- Reasoning.
- Memory.

- Emotions.
- Breathing.

Whilst most people take drugs to get 'high' some people do use Benzo's recreationally despite being a sedative as it often brings about a euphoric feeling, they sometimes mix with other drugs to get high, but with Benzo's addiction happens quickly.

For many people who are addicted, it commonly follows a legitimate prescription to treat a medical condition. However, due to the effect on the brain's chemistry, it is easy to build resilience and the required effects can only be achieved with higher doses.

The lack of professional oversight can very easily lead to addiction, it is imperative that any people taking these medications have regular reviews with their GP and only take the correct dose as prescribed. Effects of increased dosage in the short-term can include:

- Confusion and reduced cognitive function.
- Blurred vision.
- Nausea.
- Breathing difficulties.
- Amnesia.
- Coma.

Addiction and long terms use can have serious effects on your physical and mental health and can lead to hallucinations, paranoia, delusions, and seizures.

Cannabis:

Also known as marijuana, pot, weed, and by many other names, it is the most popular illicit drug in the world. 95% of students admit to trying it, with 72% of students using currently, 17% use it daily. The reasons that higher education students take cannabis can include a combination of:

- Curiosity.
- Peer pressure.
- Manging mental health issues.
- Escapism.
- Perception that it is safe.
- To get high.
- Readily available.

There is a social acceptance of cannabis that exacerbates its use, the lack of stigma means people are less likely to report others for having/using it. With students in halls being away from parents it provides an opportunity to experiment and rebel, studies also suggest students use it to tackle feelings of boredom.

The leaves of the plant are smoked to provide a feeling of relaxation, mild euphoria, mild hallucinations, and reduced anxiety. These effects can be almost instant and last several hours.

There are alternate ways to take cannabis, including consuming edibles, CBD capsules, oil, and crystals. Using bongs, vaporisers, oil rigs and more. The active chemical in Cannabis is Tetrahydrocannabinol (THC), this target certain receptors in the brain that influence perception, coordination, cognitive function, and memory.

Although there are no real short-term 'risks' of overdosing on cannabis, it does result in a high level of hospital visits due to accidents suffered whilst high. Consistent use can create dependence and addiction to cannabis is a growing concern across all age groups. In students, 1 in 6 of those who use, will go on to develop a dependence, studies suggest that 3% of male higher education students have cannabis use disorder (CUD).

We are starting to see an increase in synthetic versions of marijuana, known as K2 or spice. They are commonly a mix of herbs and spices mixed with a chemical similar to THC. These synthetic versions of the drug are more dangerous and often contain chemicals that have harmful side effects. THC withdrawal can cause the following psychological symptoms:

- Paranoia.
- Hallucinations.
- Anxiety
- Depression

An addicted person can be extremely restless and its common for them to fall out with friends, lose jobs and relationships as a result. Withdrawal can also exacerbate pre-existing conditions such as schizophrenia and increase feelings of suicide.

Despite its recreational use, one of the biggest downfalls of using cannabis is the impact on academic performance. Cannabis directly impacts your working memory and reasoning skills, and regular use has been shown through research to result in lower levels of educational attainment.

Frequent cannabis use can also result in psychotic episodes, studies show that in instances where frequent use starts at a younger age the person is twice as likely to develop a chronic psychotic disorder.

A big issue I encounter in students, halls, is that the smell given off by smoking cannabis is extremely pungent. We know most people who use cannabis, smoke in their rooms, even though this is in violation of their tenancy agreements and the law.

When burned cannabis releases hydrocarbons call terpenes that adhere to soft furnishings and fabrics, things like carpets, bedding, curtains, and mattresses. The smell is so strong it can take weeks to fade, and I have had personal experience at trying to clear the smell from a habitual user's enclosed room after they have left.

Cocaine:

Currently the third most abused drug in the UK behind alcohol and heroin. 7.7% of students surveyed have admitted using it during their time in higher education.

Cocaine is a powerful stimulant that effects your brain and body in many ways almost immediately, which forms part of its appeal. It can be snorted, smoked, or injected depending on its 'type', it works by blocking reabsorption of neurotransmitters in the brain such as serotonin and dopamine. With these remaining active and triggering the firing of nerve cells it produces an ecstatic high. The two common types of cocaine are:

Hydrochloride salt: A white powder that is commonly cut into lines and snorted or rubbed into the gums. It is also water soluble so can be dissolved and taken by injection. This type of cocaine takes longer to influence the body, it is usually known by the street names of Coke, snow, and blow.

Freebase: Has an alkaloid base, it is much less water soluble so cannot be injected but is stable at higher temperatures so can be smoked, which can bring effects much faster. The advantage of freebase cocaine is that it tends to be relatively free of impurities compared to the hydrochloride salt. Freebase Cocaine is more commonly known as 'Crack' and is cheap to produce and buy, making it popular among users. Cocaine use can lead to the following signs:

- Unnecessary hyperactivity.
- Cold symptoms, sniffing and nose bleeds.
- Increase in agitation.
- Loss of focus and concentration.
- Paranoia.
- Hallucinations.

As with most drugs cocaine use tends to impact your social life, damages relationships and jeopardises jobs. In addition, it has the potential to damage your physical and mental health.

Cocaine abuse can damage heart muscle, for people who inject endocarditis can occur (inflammation of the inner heart lining). Prolonged use can also damage kidneys. Neurological effects can be common too, many Cocaine users can have difficulty regulating moods and behaviour, decreased motor function and the inability to problem solve and complete simpler activities. Long terms effects of Cocaine use can include:

- High blood pressure, which can lead to heart failure or strokes.
- Destruction of septum and nose tissues (for those who snort).
- Severe tooth decay.
- Liver, kidney, and lung problems.
- Psychosis.
- Depression.

For students, Cocaine use can result in lower grades, use of other drugs, riskier sexual practices, PTSD, ADHD, and the most common effect of an increase in impulsivity, which when combined with lower inhibitions can have serious outcomes.

The impact on mental health for an already at-risk group is too great to ignore, the development of psychosis can happen long after the individual has stopped taking the drug.

Ecstasy:

Ecstasy is a common recreational drug usually found in pill form, it contains the chemical compound 3,4-methylenedioxy-methamphetamine (MDMA), although we are seeing illicit versions of pills that do not contain this chemical at all. In higher education 50% of students surveyed reported to have tried ecstasy, whilst 18% of students use regularly.

Ecstasy called 'Molly' or 'E' is both a psychoactive with hallucinogenic effects and a stimulant. This combination can leave you feeling euphoric and energetic whilst distorting your perceptions and sensations, it is common to enjoy tactile experiences whilst high.

It is unique in that it heightens feelings of love, empathy and sexual arousal which is part of the reason it is so popular with younger people, it is also currently popular within the gay nightclub scene.

Ecstasy floods your brain with neurotransmitters such as dopamine, serotonin, and norepinephrine. These trigger pleasure and happiness and reduce stress and depression but makes it very addictive. Coming down from the high depletes these neurotransmitters in the brain and cause the following:

- Insomnia.
- Depression.
- Anxiety.
- Confusion.
- Poor memory

As mentioned previously its common for pills marketed as Ecstasy to not contain any MDMA at all, instead they are a concoction of many varied chemicals and drugs including:

- Dextromethorphan.
- Caffeine.
- PCP.
- LSD.
- Methamphetamine.
- Cocaine.
- Heroine.

- Rat poison.
- Dog de-worming substances

Despite being commonly taken as a pill, ecstasy can also be injected, liquid versions are also available that can be ingested but these often contain GHB which is a nervous system depressant.

The key take-away from the information available on this drug is that quite often you are not taking what you think you are and can often be introducing dangerous chemicals into your body.

MDMA related deaths jumped from 8 in 2010 to 57 in 2015 in the UK, whilst the numbers do not sound significant, each one was avoidable and would have family, friends and loved ones who cared for them. The most notable incident I remember was Leah Betts who died in 1995 after taking ecstasy (although it is suggested she binge drank water to purge her system which may have contributed). Her father Paul, a former police officer became an anti-drugs campaigner giving talks at local schools. I do remember him coming to my school around that time, he was funny, engaging, and intelligent, it saddens me to learn the horrific experiences he has had since.

His work in campaigning against drugs in Essex meant he was targeted by so called 'drugs barons' who tried to kill him on two separate occasions. In 2015 he was forced to flee to Scotland, leaving his adult children and grandchildren behind.

The cost of drugs to families is incredibly high and damaging in ways you do not always expect. One of the reasons for the increase in deaths is that the dosage of MDMA found in pills has tripled from 20-

30mg in 2009 to 100mg in 2014, a trend we find with a lot of drugs in modern Britain. Therefore, it is much easier to overdose as it is harder to determine how much you are taking. Short term effects of using Ecstasy can include:

- Increased heart rate.
- Teeth clenching.
- Increased body temperature.
- Hallucinations.
- Shaking and tremors.

In the long -term prolonged use of Ecstasy can cause irreversible damage to the serotonin neurotransmitters in the brain, this can lead to difficulty in sleeping, absorbing new information and processing emotions.

Ketamine:

Ketamine, 'K' or 'Special K' is a dissociative aesthetic. It can be used as a date rape drug due to the paralysis it causes. It is common in veterinary medicine, often as a tranquiliser of large mammals. It comes in the form of white powder but is also available in pill form and a liquid (which makes it easier to slip into drinks).

The dissociative effects of Ketamine are so strong that not only does it cause temporary paralysis, but it also causes visual and auditory hallucinations. It reduces physical sensations, but the user remains awake, which is why it is popular among those experiencing physical and emotional pain. The effects of taking this drug can be unpredictable, for many it comes with the sense of euphoria, however the hallucinations can sometimes be frightening.

When mixed with other 'depressant' drugs such as alcohol it can cause respiratory depression which can result in death. Given the drug also causes a temporary paralysis people struggle to clear their airways which can lead to choking and suffocation.

LSD:

Lysergic acid diethylamide (LSD) is an odourless liquid chemical often called 'Acid'; it is sold in tiny amounts on blotted paper called tabs. On average a person will try LSD for the first time around the age of 20, usually within a college or university environment.

Thankfully its less common that it was in the 1960s and 1970s. It is a powerful hallucinogenic that affects the serotonin levels in the brain, this controls, mood, senses, memory, and perception of pain. It also distorts your view of reality; this is referred to as 'tripping'.

LSD can increase your body temperature and heart rate, it energises you, but you can also feel confused, anxious, and overwhelmed. It can take anywhere up to 2 hours to affect you once taken, but effects can last anywhere between 6 – 12 hours, during which you can experience a wide range of emotions. Every trip is unique which makes it hard to predict, some trips will be mild, others will trigger anxiety, panic, paranoia, and anger.

The feelings and visions brought on by hallucinations can make people act out in very violent and dangerous ways and since the trip lasts so long, it can be almost impossible to carry out normal activities. Some users will experience flashbacks of hallucinations, and mood swings even after the drug has left their system, this can happen, days months or even a year after. Frequent use can also trigger psychosis.

Risks associated with taking LSD can include self-harm if user has pre-existing depression and anxiety. Whilst it is said that LSD does no physical harm to the body, it can cause many psychological problems that leads to harm: either self-harm or violence to others.

Nitrous oxide:

Often called 'Nos' or 'laughing gas', nitrous oxide is an anaesthetic gas and an anxiety and pain reliever. It has a long history of being used in medicine for this reason, more commonly in dentistry and midwifery. Due to it being historically readily available and legal to buy as it is a key component to make whipping cream, it is often used recreationally and evidenced by discarded small metal cylinders.

In 2019/20 half a million people in the UK admitted to taking Nitrous oxide and is the second most used drug for 16–24-year-olds (8.7%). In 2016 the sale of Nitrous Oxide was made illegal to buy in the UK in the psychoactive substances act. However, it is not a crime to possess.

As mentioned, Nitrous oxide can be found in whipped cream chargers; finger length metal cylinders that contain around 8g of pressurised Nitrous oxide, which is a colourless sweet tasting gas. It is discharged into a balloon using a 'cracker' and inhaled to bring about a rush of dizziness and euphoria (which is why people laugh). Sounds can be distorted and hallucinations, although less common, can occur. As it is an anaesthetic people can fall over and appear drunk when high, although highs can fade in as little as two minutes.

Due to this, it is common for people to take many hits over a short time, however, the gas from the balloon displaces the air in your lungs and can prevent oxygenation, as a result limbs may feel heavy and tingly, and the heart rate will increase. The combination of an overdose of Nitrous and lack of oxygen can cause the following issues:

- Anaemia.
- Vitamin B12 deficiency.
- Tight chest and difficulty breathing.
- Hallucinations and psychosis.
- Increased blood pressure.
- Increased risk of heart attack or stroke.
- Seizures.
- Brain damage.

It is not recommended to inhale from other sources as it can cause oxygen deprivation and death, nitrous tanks used in car racing contains sulphur dioxide which can cause harm to the body. On average 5 people a year die from abusing Nitrous oxide, those who use it over a long time can start to develop depression, tiredness, and forgetfulness.

Psilocybin:

Psilocybin is the active ingredient in magic mushrooms, when taken orally it is quickly metabolised into Psilocin which affects the serotonin receptors in the brain. Much like LSD it is a psychedelic that can trigger hallucinations.

The benefit of Psilocybin is that at controlled doses (8-25 mg orally) it is considered safe for humans and is the subject of study into its effects on depression. It is believed that certain receptors in the brain become overactive during depression and that Psilocybin can disrupt these receptors giving them a chance to reform.

According to some surveys as many as 30% of students have tried magic mushrooms (shrooms). Whilst many who try magic mushrooms only do so the once out of curiosity, many long-term users are likely to abuse alcohol or other drugs such as LSD as well. Magic mushrooms can be taken fresh or dried, they can be eaten on their own, mixed with other food or brewed into a tea.

The effects start to begin around 30-45 minutes after ingestion and can last up to 6 hours. A mild trip may leave a person feeling relaxed or drowsy/sleepy, however a stronger dose may trigger hallucinations, paranoia, and anxiety. Extreme doses and long-term use can trigger psychosis.

Every trip is unpredictable and unique, some trips may be enjoyable and relaxing, whilst others can induce panic attacks, paranoia, and a fear of losing control. Side effects can include:

- Nausea and vomiting.
- Stomach cramps and diarrhoea.
- Increased heart rate and blood pressure.

- Increased temperature.
- Lack of coordination.
- Dilated pupils.
- Drowsiness.

In more extreme case there are risks to mental health and if taken in large enough doses the side effects can lead to death.

As it is impossible to tell how 'strong' a mushroom is, it is extremely difficult to monitor your dosage, as a result it can be very difficult to overdose. Also being a mushroom, it can be difficult to know if you are taking the right type, as several mushroom types are poisonous to humans and can trigger sever illness and even death.

Study/smart drugs:

Also called nootropics, studies show that around 10-15% of UK higher education students have used study drugs regularly, at least once and 7% use them regularly, but this number is on the rise worldwide. More and more people are using drugs to boost memory, concentration, and mental performance for academic purposes, this is known in the medical community as pharmacological cognitive enhancement (PCE).

Common forms of drug used this way are Adderall, Ritalin (for treating ADHD) and Modafinil (sleep disorder drug). Of those who use them, nearly 60% are obtaining them through friends, family or abusing their own prescriptions.

Whilst many of these drugs are not harmful in the short term, there is some concern about long term misuse leading to cognitive impairment, anxiety, weight gain, increased blood pressure and the triggering of dormant mental health illnesses.

Most students who use illegal or non-prescribed drugs do not know the correct dosage and can often take amounts in excess of standard levels. Students who are focussed on short-term benefits such as exam results may take much higher doses which can lead to overdoses and dependency.

Political plan:

The current government strategic plan is to break drug supply chains and establish a world class treatment and recovery system, although what they say and what they do are two very different things. In the political sphere the issue of drugs is often tackled with a binary approach, either through a tough crackdown or complete liberalisation. Although the last UK prime minister says there is no evidence that decriminalisation is the right thing to do currently.

Decriminalisation does not make things legal, but rather does not criminalise them, and when we consider that many drugs' offences are considered minor offences (possession, possession of paraphernalia etc), this could relieve the burden on police and the justice system. Although every idea has unintended consequences and decriminalisation could engender a social de-stigmatisation and increase drug use, which in my opinion is not desirable either.

Portugal decriminalised all drugs in 2001 after a spate of drug related deaths and invested in public health. They saw a fall in death, disease, and overall social costs, I suspect as people did not have to fear being criminalised and could ask for medical help, clean needles and so on.

Spain And Switzerland has safe injection rooms for intravenous drug users and most countries provide safe needles free of charge.

The all-out war on drugs championed by politicians has barely changed, the same rhetoric has been used for decades but our politicians have not delivered. Perhaps it is time for a new approach to tackling drugs?

In terms of students the biggest risks to health via drug use we see are:

- Misuse/abuse and overdosing.
- Mixing drugs and alcohol (or different drugs).
- Assaults and injuries whilst under the influence.
- Initiation ceremonies.

If drugs were decriminalised, we could ensure students have the correct advice without being prosecuted or losing their university place, as the social stigma can cause people to hide their drug use due to fear or shame.

With criminals determining the dosage of drugs brought illegally and often cutting them with dangerous chemicals, it can be difficult for users to know the purity of their drugs, if there are any dangerous additives or how much they should take.

Netherlands was the first country to have trialled drug testing to save lives, where people can go and have the purity of their drugs determined prior to taking them. Other western countries have since followed suit, even if drugs remain criminalised.

The illegality of drugs can often be a large part of initiation ceremonies and can be tempting for young rebellious teenagers fresh out of the family home, decriminalisation could prevent this, although there is a legitimate fear it could also increase drug use among this age group.

Law:

Whatever our thoughts are on what should be, we must operate on what the law currently says. Currently one of the largest pieces of legislation in this area is the Misuse of drugs act 1971. This covers the following areas:
- Possession of controlled drugs (section 5)
- Possession with intent to supply (section 4/5)
- Supply on controlled drugs (section 4)
- Production of controlled drugs (section 4)
- Cultivation of cannabis (section 6)
- Occupiers' liability (section 8)

If the police have reasonable grounds, they can search a person or vehicle and detain evidence of drugs or paraphernalia, this power comes from Section 23 of the misuse of drugs act 1971 and the Police and Criminal evidence act 1984 (PACE).

If you are found with drugs, police can obtain a warrant to search your home/property, which includes your student accommodation. Within 1 month of warrant being obtained, they can enter and search your premises, search anyone at the premises and seize and detain drugs or documents.

Police can only enter premises without a warrant if a serious or dangerous incident has taken place. Situations in which the police can enter premises without a warrant include:

- Dealing with a breach of the peace or prevent it.
- To enforce an arrest warrant.
- To arrest a person in connection with certain offences.
- To recapture someone who has escaped from custody.
- To save life or prevent serious damage to property.

Apart from when they are preventing significant injury to life or property, the police must have reasonable grounds for believing that the person they are looking to arrest is on the premises. If the police do arrest you, they can also enter and search any premises where you were during or immediately before the arrest. However, they can search only for evidence relating to the offence for which you have been arrested, and they must have reasonable grounds for believing there is evidence there. They can also search any room occupied by someone who is under arrest for certain serious offences and universities

Matthew J. Evans

would be obliged to allow them access. Again, the
police officer who carries out the search must have
reasonable grounds for suspecting that there is
evidence on the premises relating to the offence or a
similar offence.

In all other circumstances, the police must
have a search warrant before they can enter your
home. They should enter the property at a reasonable
hour unless this would frustrate their search. When
the occupier is present, the police must ask for
permission to search the property – again, unless it
would frustrate the search to do this.

Police do have a general power of seizure
under PACE, if police are lawfully on your premises,
they have the power to seize anything on reasonable
grounds if

- It is obtained as the result of an offence.
- Necessary to seize it to prevent it being
  concealed, lost, damaged, altered or destroyed.

University security staff will have their own policies
and procedures for dealing with students suspected to
be in possession of drugs but will usually involve the
police.

Country lines:

This is not a new issue; it is a form of criminal
exploitation that involves forcing many young people
to carry drugs across the country. They do this by
befriending vulnerable children and adults online and
then manipulate them into drug dealing or to deliver
drugs to areas outside of their hometowns and
counties, all controlled by dedicated mobile phones or

Matthew J. Evans

would be obliged to allow them access. Again, the police officer who carries out the search must have reasonable grounds for suspecting that there is evidence on the premises relating to the offence or a similar offence.

In all other circumstances, the police must have a search warrant before they can enter your home. They should enter the property at a reasonable hour unless this would frustrate their search. When the occupier is present, the police must ask for permission to search the property – again, unless it would frustrate the search to do this.

Police do have a general power of seizure under PACE, if police are lawfully on your premises, they have the power to seize anything on reasonable grounds if

- It is obtained as the result of an offence.
- Necessary to seize it to prevent it being concealed, lost, damaged, altered or destroyed.

University security staff will have their own policies and procedures for dealing with students suspected to be in possession of drugs but will usually involve the police.

County lines:

This is not a new issue; it is a form of criminal exploitation that involves forcing many young people to carry drugs across the country. They do this by befriending vulnerable children and adults online and then manipulate them into drug dealing or to deliver drugs to areas outside of their hometowns and counties, all controlled by dedicated mobile phones or

139

'drug lines'. Unfortunately, county lines exist everywhere, some areas get more press coverage, but 90% of police forces have reported county lines activity in their area.

Young people aged 14-17 are the most likely group to be targeted by these criminals, however children as young as 7 and young adults have been groomed into this lifestyle too.

There are concerns that student accommodation can be used to deal drugs and that students are being brough into the county lines web. Where there is a market for drugs there will be a county lines operation. The criminal gangs will be looking out for vulnerable students, or students with debt they will be looking to pay off by selling drugs. These students often end up in debt bondage, usually of a result of their own drug use debt.

County lines criminals are transient and adaptive in their methods, a common practice is for them to 'cuckoo', to take over someone's home and use it to deal, store or take drugs and even live there temporarily themselves. Common signs of Cuckooing include:

- Increase in people entering and leaving the property at strange times.
- Increase in vehicle activity at the property.
- Increase in anti-social behaviour
- Have not seen the person who lives there but have seen others in the room.

These indicators are less noticeable in student halls of accommodation, with many signs being excused as normal student life/behaviour. This allows the county lines to continue operating for longer periods. More obvious signs to watch for would be:

- Witnessing drug dealing.
- Unknown or suspicious looking characters hanging around on campus.
- Do other students have gang affiliations?
- Do others only use nicknames when referring to others?
- Have they access to multiple phones and receive many calls and texts.

Other county lines gangs have begun to enrol on university courses at different institutions across the UK to sell drugs to students. They infiltrate campuses, set up local networks, and use their status as students to avoid arrest and suspicion. If you have any concerns regarding drug dealing or county lines, you can speak to your housing manager or call the police on 101.

Dark web:

Like how students become victims of debt bondage under county lines activity, some drug using students find out how to order drugs online, this makes it safer, cheaper, and more convenient. They quickly discover they could buy extra and sell the excess to their friends to help pay for tuition. This can spiral out of control and before you know it have several thousands of pounds worth of drugs in their possession (in their room).

Crypto markets on the dark web offer a convenient and safe way to purchase drugs online. It is thought of those who buy this way, the majority are young males, who attend the club scene. These buyers will tend to have a wider range of drugs than other drug users and these will be a lower price and of greater quality than previous dealers.

Drug buyers access the dark web by means of 'the onion router' (TOR), this uses many layers of encryption to ensure personal information is secure and individuals cannot be tracked. They would then access selling sites akin to eBay, where many black-market goods can be sold including but not limited to drugs, weapons, stolen credit card details, forged documents, and counterfeit currency. These products are bought and sold using a cryptocurrency such as bitcoin.

The first big drugs marketplace was 'silk road' created by Ross Ulbricht aka 'Dread Pirate Roberts' in February of 2011, two and a half years later it was eventually shut down, but not before processing $9 billion of drugs sales, of which 10% went to the sites founder. Since the shutting down of silk road, many new sites have opened, creating a multi-billion-dollar market across the world. With so many drugs arriving by mail, your average postman has unknowingly become the largest drug dealer in town.

Since the dark web exists outside of the law, there have been many fraudulent markets and scammers who set up fake sites to steal money from buyers. Also, drugs gangs often fund other, more serious crimes from the proceeds of drugs, and you are unwittingly funding these crimes by buying drugs.

The eBay like nature of the sites means that buyers tend to buy a wider range of drugs, buying what is on offer to 'give it a try' or sell to friends.

This can lead to people overdosing by mixing drugs and most overdoses and fatalities are a result of poly-drug use.

Whilst drugs like Cannabis have little social stigma, they can also become a gateway to something much more addictive and dangerous, in my own teen years, my friends and I smoked pot regularly. However, one or two members of the group later went on to try pills and then powder.

Stay away from the slippery slope, just say no to drugs.

Personal safety.

Around a third of university students in the UK become the victims of crime, the majority being theft and burglary, approximately 20% of robberies will happen within the first six weeks. I suspect this is entirely intentional as most students will have valuable belongings and more disposable cash at this time than at any other point in their student life.

Thieves will be looking for expensive equipment, televisions, games consoles, phones, watches, tablets, and laptops even prescription drugs. Smaller items that can be easily hidden and readily resold are ideal for thieves looking to make a quick deal.

You should check insurance details of the institute to determine what is covered, any specifics which may affect your chances of a claim should you fall victim to thieves, you may want to consider adding your own private insurance cover for peace of mind. Invest in an ultraviolet marker or electronic tagging to ensure your devices can be located and returned to you.

The immobilise website allows you to recover your valuables by marking them, tagging them with a microchip or using electronic RFID tagging. These items are registered to you online and if found they will be returned to you.

Mobile device security.

As most people will admit, our phones are not just devices for making calls on anymore. They are our calendars, alarm clocks, and debit cards (via e-Pay). We use them to check emails, surf the web, use social media, for maps, apps, dating and more. They are miniature computers in our pockets that hold valuable details of our lives and our friends and families. This information is just as confidential as the information on our laptops or personal computers.

To prevent 'losing' your phone and important information you should use software that prevents unauthorised use of your phone. A good example would be Norton mobile security, this not only prevents strangers from using your phone, but will also help the police to locate it.

Additionally mobile security software allows the user (you) to lock your phone remotely via the internet and can display a message written by you to notify anyone who 'finds' it to return it to you. If the phone is unrecoverable and/or stolen Norton mobile security will allow you to delete data remotely so that your personal information cannot be used by anyone else. Other safety tips include:

- Do not use public Wi-fi, these are unsecured and easy modes for hackers to gain access to your data.

- Back up data by syncing it to your laptop at home, do not use your phone as long-term storage.

- Research apps before downloading them, you could be installing malware in your device and doing the thieves job for them.

- When discarding old phones, reset them to factory settings first to remove personal data.

As mentioned, phones are miniature computers and are not immune to hacking, malware, or viruses. Phishing is just as much an issue for mobile phones as it is computers. Use the same vigilance on your phone as you would your computer and do not click on unknown links.

Norton mobile security mentioned above will protect your phone from phishing and remove threats before they cause any harm. Other mobile device services are available, I use Norton as an example as I have used them in the past.

Bike Theft.

In many university cities, bikes are very popular, and bike theft is growing. Data released by cycling UK shows that among university cities in the UK, Cambridge has the highest rate of bike thefts reported by students, with 1747 reported between April 2020 and March 2021, with 38000 students in the city this means one in every 22 students has experienced bike thefts.

Bristol follows closely behind with 1612, Oxford, Leeds and Birmingham all had over 1000 bike thefts in the same period.

Of over 9000 thefts in that year in the UK (reported by students), only 13 (0.15%) resulted in a suspect being charged or cautioned for theft.

The data included the areas from which the bikes were stolen, the highest risk areas are:

- Parking areas: 19.3%

- Education building: 18.6%
- Supermarket: 14.8%
- Shopping area: 14.2%

As you can see, these are areas frequented by students the most, you should never assume a bike is safe if left unlocked. Take the time to make sure it is secure before going shopping or going to class.

Most tenancy agreements will not allow you to store bikes inside rooms or flats, so you will have to leave them outside chained to bike racks. Ensure you leave them in the safest place, look for well-lit areas within sight of an active CCTV camera. Use the appropriate locks, a D-lock is far safer than a chain that can be cut and are available from most bike/accessory shops.

Make sure you oil the keylock on your D-lock regularly to avoid it rusting over, there is nothing more frustrating and embarrassing than having to steal your own bike. If this does happen you may have to ask university maintenance to help remove your bike, I have allowed this on occasion before, and would always ask for proof of ownership. Ensure you have a receipt and a few pictures with you and the bike as further evidence.

Alternatively, and more importantly, having it registered on immobilise with an electronic RFID tag is very good evidence of ownership. Whilst you cannot guarantee it will not get stolen, you can make it as hard as possible for thieves and make it as easy as possible to get it returned to you.

Room keys:

When you sign your tenancy agreement on arrival at your institution, you will be given a set of keys, in many instances these will have a tag or be marked with your room/building number. Once you are familiar with the area, you will want to remove this tag as soon as possible, either return it to the residential management team or keep it in a drawer until the end of your tenancy.

We all have made mistakes where we have left our keys somewhere, lost a bag or left them in a jacket pocket. If someone finds a set of keys and they have an address written on them, you are opening yourself to opportunistic burglaries.

Furthermore, where an institute may charge you to print a new key, if you have left the tag on, they may have no choice but to replace the locks, leaving you out of pocket far more than necessary.

Identity theft:

Criminals can use your personal details to create another 'you', all they need is your name, address, and date of birth. With this information, they can open new bank accounts, apply for credit cards and so on. Some warning signs that you may be the victim of identity theft include:

- You have lost important documents, or they have been stolen, such as driving licence or passport.
- Mail from your bank does not arrive.
- Items that you do not recognise appear on your credit card or bank statements.

- You receive letters from debt collectors for debts that are not yours.

To reduce the risk of becoming a victim of identity theft you should shred any old documents showing your name, address, and other personal details. In the absence of your own shredder, you can ask in your faculty admin office to use theirs. Other methods include:

- Redirecting mail when moving house.
- Store any personal documents in a safe and secure place.
- Monitor your credit card and bank statements regularly.

Part Three:
Stronger student.

Student life can be overwhelming, living away from home, workload, deadlines, making new friends and the worries of finances, budgeting and having to find work. It is hard to keep ownership of your mental wellbeing alongside these other issues, but there are some simple ways you can learn to take control.

Mental health is a growing concern among the student population, with a greater number of students reporting anxiety and depression than ever before. We need to take this subject seriously, even if you do not have a history of mental health disorders.

Stress, anxiety and depression can affect everyone and in this section, I will discuss self-care, setting boundaries and how to avoid the victim mentality, all around a core idea of resilience and its importance to young adults.

Resilience.

Resilience is best described as growing a thick skin and not letting things upset you, it starts as a choice, but becomes a habit. To describe resilience and the victim mentality I am going to start by discussing my own experiences.

As a child of the early Eighties, the middle of three brothers born over three years, growing up was a hugely different experience to what children face today. We did not have internet until the mid-nineties and there were few video games, and no tablets or phones to play on, we had to go out and enjoy the world, even at an early age and often unsupervised.

My birth parents separated at the end of '83 and my mother had a tough time managing alone with three young children, she cut a lot of corners to make ends meet but had one too many brushes with the law and unfortunately this resulted in my brothers, and I being taken into the care system. Months later, due to an injury suffered by my older brother whilst in care, my mother was able to challenge the system and reclaim her parental rights. It also helped that she had met and moved in with a new man who moved to the area in search of work and could provide some stability.

My brothers and I, however, did not receive a good role model in our stepfather, he was a heavy-handed disciplinarian who filled us with fear, he had many character flaws, which impacted his ability to be an appropriate father figure.

My mother was a housewife and home maker, she barely worked and relied on the income of my stepfather who sadly through the financial 'crash' of '85 lost his house and shortly after, through health issues could no longer work, my mother developed her own health issues over time also.

We grew up a family on benefits, raised in council housing in rough areas of the town in which we lived (one year our house was burgled, and our Christmas presents were stolen, on another occasion a man was savagely beaten and suffered brain damage outside our house). We wore matching clothes my grandmother made from old curtains, had our heads shaved by our neighbour because we often could not afford haircuts and we wore hand me down school uniform from cousins that had more holes than a politician's police statement.

Needless to say, we were bullied, a lot! And kids can be cruel. As we were boys, this meant physical attacks as well as mental bullying that continued for years. It would be fair to say at times all my brothers and I had were each other, and even then, sometimes not even that. As we grew older my younger brother started to develop mental health problems that exhibited as uncontrollable rage, usually targeted at us.

Personally, like many people I had individual challenges to deal with, I was born with congenital talipes equinovarus (CTEV), more commonly known as bilateral club foot. This meant periods of having my legs in plaster cast, physiotherapy, wheelchair use and when I was around 10 the best part of a year wearing metal callipers on my legs (I was Forrest Gump a year or two before Tom Hanks). I had a lot of time away from school and thankfully spent much of that with grandparents to take some pressure off my parents, it was this time that led to my love of reading and other hobbies, and I consumed books en-masse. I treasured time with my grandparents, it was time away from school, home and I was with people who gave me their time.

At an early age I had to start wearing glasses, which did not help with the bullies. Due to my family being on benefits, I could only pick from a limited number of 'free' NHS glasses, they were hideous, but beggars cannot be choosers. I was also very accident prone; At eleven, I cut my hand open (almost in half straight down) and had to learn to write left-handed for a year. At thirteen a concrete bollard fell on me, which has led to over a dozen surgeries to correct the damage done to my foot over my lifetime. I also have periods of severe hip pain because of my congenital defects.

Looking back at my childhood I can see where my character flaws developed, I learned to lie to avoid being punished by my stepfather, I was overly emotional and had periods of depression due to bullying. Whilst I never gave up, I never thought of suicide I was very much the victim, objectively and mentally. This impacted the way I acted and viewed the world and made things worse, the more I acted as a victim, the more people treated me as such, I was an easy target.

Despite my shortcomings I did not let my physical issues stop me from trying to compete in cross country and rugby for my school, and later Sunday league football as an adult (almost unthinkable as a child constantly in plaster casts). Although an

ACL rupture whilst paintballing in my twenties and my hip problems has really limited my ability to take part in sports as I have gotten older.

Of course, the bullying did not stop at childhood. In middle school and into high school, it continued, it was an ever-present weight dragging me down through my formative years. When I was not dealing with it in school, there were issues at home.

It led to me entering toxic friendships, thankful for any attention, time away from school and home, even though some of them were not acting in good faith and would use me as a clown to keep around and make fun of, or to exclude and fetch the ball during ball games.

There was one good friend, a guy who despite being extremely popular at school, still considered himself 'apart' (he was black and Jehovah's witness and had experienced some bigotry due to this), I think he understood me as being an outcast and despite also being friends with popular people who did not like me, he gave me time.

My older brother, my Irish twin, was my rock throughout most of my childhood, the strong male figure I never really had. When he was thirteen, he learned the hard way how to defend himself and realised he had an inner strength and capacity for violence that scared a lot of 'would be' bullies. He grew up quickly. I was able to hide in his shadow for a time to avoid some of the worst bullying, but he was not always around, and it continued until the day I decided to stand up for myself. It was the toughest thing I had to do, and honestly was not what I wanted even though my older brother told me it was the best course of action.

It was scary, what would happen if I got beat up? Would the bullying get worse? In that difficult moment I learned that I too had some inner courage, although no real capacity or will to be violent unless it was necessary and a last resort. Violence did not come easy to me, but I would not let that prevent me from standing up for myself, eventually the fear of getting hurt lessened.

Things got better for a while, as a young teenager, in school I joined the chess team, met two great friends, Samuel, and Jay (names changed to provide anonymity), I left old unhealthy friendships behind, I had my first girlfriend and my first heartbreak; all the things' teenagers should experience. However, when I was Fourteen my older brother fell ill, an infection that damaged his kidneys, he was in hospital for some time and had an allergic reaction to the penicillin they gave him to fight the infection. The scariest point in my life, was my mum taking that phone call from the hospital, saying we needed to go and say goodbye as he was going to die, I will never forget that moment for as long as I live.

Thankfully, that did not happen, against all odds he survived and recovered, although lost a lot of weight in the process. Things changed for him after that, he became a different person, he fell in with some bad people, left school at 16 to work, he drank, smoked, and philandered his way through his teenage years into adulthood.

For myself I developed a thick outer shell, I became the class clown, all jokes and silliness on the outside, but inside full of self-doubt, fear, and a bag of emotions. This was my survival mechanism, and it is still true to this day, albeit with less fear and emotion.

Facing high school and sixth form without my older brother to protect me was tough, but necessary, I think. Sadly, there was a large group of people the year below me who fancied themselves a 'gang' and I frequently caught their attention. After everything I had been through, I became a victim again. How could I stand up for myself against such odds? I did not know what to do.

I did not realise it at the time, but victimhood is a mentality, it changed the way I carried myself, the way I spoke and cowered, always looked down with sunken shoulders. What I did not know then but know now, is that when you act and think like a victim, people treat you that way.

In addition to the numerous physical assaults from this group, I was also the victim of a serious assault from young men from the local travelling community. In defending a female classmate who was being sexually harassed, by standing up to them, I became the target for their anger.

Thinking back, I know I did the right thing and would do it again, even knowing the cost. As I said before, lacking courage was not my problem, but I will never understand why it took me so long to stand up for myself against that gang (which I did eventually).

In my final sixth form year, a chance encounter changed my life for the better, a friend suggested I take up a course being offered during a social week, it was a self-defence class. When I arrived, I knew a couple of people from previous social groups I attended in middle school, they were led by a small woman in her fifties. She was small in height, but height alone, being with her for only a few minutes, I realised she was a strong no-nonsense, iron-willed independent woman, who you certainly did not mess with. I liked her instantly. Due to my previous associations, she invited me to join her group outside of school, I accepted and what I learned in those following years became a corner stone of the person I am today.

After sixth form, I got accepted to university, but did not have the money or support to go, so instead I took a year out and looked for work, hoping to save. Things at home deteriorated during this time though, my mother and stepfather separated, my mother and younger brother moved into a hostel, I moved in with my then girlfriends' family.

My stepfather had a mental health break, trying many times to commit suicide and on one occasion trying to kill my older brother, attacking him with a kitchen knife. Everything fell apart! My older brother left home and moved in across the road with a 'friend' who as it later turned out was a drug dealer who groomed him via drug debt, and we all left our stepfather for good.

With having to support rent and living with a girlfriend, saving for university proved impossible, so I did not go and gave up the dream of academia, instead I began working in a factory. As much as it bothers me not to have that opportunity, I do not regret this, I met two good men who proved essential to my personal development and looking back I cannot thank them enough.

In my private time I worked with my self-defence instructor, I had established new paternal and maternal figures in my life, strong ones who had good values and gave me the time and support I needed.

With the breakup of my family home, the relationship with my mother and older brother deteriorated. My biggest regret is losing my older brother during that time. We were both stubborn, however there was a lot going on in his personal life which I think were irreconcilable, and unfortunately led to him going to prison for drugs offences. Surprisingly, the phone call he made on his first night in prison was to me. We were able to talk often during this time, and I supported him as much as I could throughout his sentence. Strangely it healed the rift and over time, brought us back together.

My relationship with my then girlfriend eventually broke down, teenage love is rarely built to last, she began a relationship with a co-worker whilst we were together, and I ended up homeless as a result. Thankfully it was not for too long, I was able to sofa surf with family before finding my feet and meeting a new woman, a good woman, my now wife of nearly twenty years.

My brother served his time and we patched up our relationship, however as so frequently happened, the good was accompanied by the bad, shortly after my good friend Jay committed suicide, he hung himself in his garage and was found by our friend Samuel. This was a terrible time for all of us, Jay had a rough childhood too and after a string of family deaths and personal problems must have felt he could not go on. I just wish he would have talked to us about it, and I often feel guilt, thinking back at missed opportunities to help that I did not see at the time. He is still in my thoughts a decade and a half later.

Life became easier as I got older, I spent a decade as a self-defence instructor, during this time I also worked within the security industry. I was able to learn and apply much to the way I acted and reacted, the way I carried myself, my habits and who I let into my life. Due to this I have never felt like a victim and have never been attacked or bullied since.

I have worked as a welfare officer for the FA, ran fundraising for a football team and championed charity events. For the past decade I have worked at a university, more recently in student accommodation, specialising in student discipline and pastoral care and I see first-hand the troubles that students get into.

I do not look for, or want pity, I am no longer a victim and there are many who have worse childhoods, including Jay. I have discussed my background here so that you understand many people have baggage and struggles, even those you would not normally assume. People are not born strong, confident, weak or victims, it is all learned behaviour. Even bullies have their own baggage, studies show that 60% of people who bully have experienced physical, mental, or sexual abuse from within their household. It appears that suffering seeks companionship.

I am hoping that like me, many people, even those with challenging backgrounds, can grow to become better versions of themselves, can avoid being the 'victim'.

Another point I want to make, is despite how my childhood sounds, there were good people there, and it is easy to miss them, especially if your too consumed in self-pity. The woman who took my brothers and I in when we were in the care system, she was a good person, had a generous heart, and despite having children of her own, opened her home to three young boys who had a bad time. Ok my brother got hurt, but children play hard, and accidents happen, it was not her fault (he ran into a table).

Afterwards a man who having only known my mother for a short time took us in. I have full respect for men who are willing to take on and raise another person's children, being a stepparent is not easy and it is amazing to see people taking on responsibility as opposed to shirking it. I know many stepfathers and it gives me a sense of inner joy and faith in people that I cannot adequately voice at this time, children are our legacy. Whilst that did not end well for us it does for many others.

I think of the 'friends' who stood by me, when they did not have to, they wanted to have me around. I think of the adult figures in my life who were willing to give me time, the cumulation of which has made me the man I am today.

I am not perfect by any means, but the way I see the world and how others see me is much healthier now. And that is key, learning to see positives and look forward rather than back is so important to good mental health.

Today I am happily married, have a good career, I am finally studying for a degree and have three wonderful children. I maintain a close relationship with my older brother and have many friends from a diverse group of people, and two very special friendships, akin to brothers even, everything I could have dreamed of as a child.

I still have my flaws and character defects, no-one is perfect, but we can always be better. And the challenges and sacrifices still occur. Like many currently, it is a challenge to provide for my family, but I take on that responsibility, own it and try my best, it is difficult, but I draw great meaning from my responsibilities.

My children will never know the hardships I faced, but their own experiences are terrifying and unique, and I hope I can guide them through it. Considering the start I had, I consider my children my success, I will likely never be a millionaire or famous, but I have built something that will outlive me. Whilst it is easy to focus on the losses and missed opportunities, in many ways I feel like a winner.

If I could boil the lessons of my life story down to two words, they would be resilience and responsibility. Unfortunately, I did not learn these lessons until much later, but such is life, the best lessons are learned from self-reflection, but learning from the mistakes of others would be preferable.

Resilience is not something that can come straight away, it takes a lot to face your fears. Doing the right thing, being assertive and telling the truth even though the consequences could be harsh, has to become a habit.

You must try to see the positives in life, bad things happen, you can either make changes or accept them and move forward, the worst thing you can do is turn your energy inwards and become a victim.

Victim mentality.

Whilst I will discuss victim mentality in more depth here, it is important to distinguish between being an objective victim and having a victim mentality. Many people do experience crimes, physical violence, sexual assault, and childhood trauma, in most cases this was beyond their control and to try to accept personal responsibility for the actions of others would be unhealthy and pointless.

There are times in all our lives when we get lost in self-pity, feeling sorry for ourselves because of a bereavement, loss of a family pet or even a divorce. We feel powerless and feel sorry for ourselves. This is normal and usually temporary, the victim mentality however is forming an identity around the status of victim and becoming reliant on the pity from yourself and others. It is not something that happened to you, it is who you are. You do not move on from trauma, you hold onto it, telling the story repeatedly until you are lost in the mindset, paralysed.

The victim mentality normally presents itself in our actions and attitudes. If you anger or offend easily, do not take responsibility for your actions, and you constantly make excuses and blame others, you have likely fallen foul of it (and most of us do at some point, especially when we are young).

For many, they feel they have had a particularly tough life and no matter how hard they try, they just cannot get ahead. The world is a terrible, dangerous, and oppressive monster that they cannot defeat. We have all been hurt in some shape or form and we carry that pain and past experiences with us, it shapes who we become and is part of our identities, but it does not have to define us, at least not negatively.

The issue is that the victim mentality has benefits to us in the short term. You do not need to take responsibility; you get lots of attention and sympathy and you get a righteous feeling that your negative emotions are someone else's fault. People will refrain from criticising you; they will pity you, feel they need to help and give you attention.

It turns our negative aspects into a virtue, for you view the world through a binary lens of good and bad, you are the innocent party, and the bad things are the external oppressive force. It is like a drug, addictive yet toxic. You get lots of benefit without any real short-term cost. Of course, in the long-term people start to see you as a toxic person, constantly whining, complaining, and shirking responsibility and that is no good for keeping or making friends.

We are starting to see what happens when large groups adopt victim mentality, it creates a positive feedback loop of sympathy and reinforcement, although after a time, they start to outdo each other about who is more victimised and more deserving of sympathy, an intersectionality of oppression.

Modern day therapists use an approach called CBT to combat serious depression and anxiety: cognitive behavioural therapy. In which you learn to recognise and discover the extreme thoughts which lead you to feel depressed or anxious, where you catastrophise, over generalise or exhibit binary thinking. Researchers in the 1960s realised that if you can correct these thoughts, you free the individual from the negative emotions attached and you break the feedback loop.

Unfortunately, elements in today's societies have forgotten these lessons and seem to reinforce these cognitive failings through "safe spaces" and banning of certain topics or discussions that can be deemed 'harmful' to people's feelings. American social psychologist Johnathon Haidt discusses this very issue in his book 'coddling of the American mind'. He points out that our mental health works much like our immune system, if you 'wrap a child in cotton wool', coddle them, you remove opportunities to develop immunity to bacteria and viruses. By removing 'harmful' words from the environment you remove the opportunity for people to develop immunity to them, it is as Nietzsche says, "what doesn't kill you makes you stronger". Without these challenges to the safe space systems, we will never throw off the victim mentality.

Adversity leads to strength, to quote Greek philosopher Herodes Atticus "I have never met a strong person with an easy past". It reminds me of the story of George St-Pierre who was bullied relentlessly as a child. He overcame his past and went on to become the UFC champion, he used his past experiences to grow as a person, to become stronger.

Ultimately, we have choices. When giving into the victim mentality we choose to not take responsibility for our behaviour, it is the easy way out. The first step to recovery is to understand you made a choice to adopt a victim mentality, but you can choose not to and instead choose to take control of how you respond to life's challenges.

Do not react: When you let your emotions dictate how you react, you have already lost control of the situation. Take a breath before reacting, try not to make emotional decisions and ask yourself if there is a wiser course of action. This is old wisdom, parents from when I was young would always insist you 'count to ten' before reacting to someone who had upset you.

Be thankful: There may be areas where we struggle, but there are areas where we are blessed too. It did not matter how poor I was if I had my wife and children around me, food on the table and a roof above our heads. We would make do! Be thankful for what we have, appreciate those who help us and then work hard to resolve our issues, this will keep our outlook positive. Psychological studies indicate positive thinking improves the memory of positive experiences.

Apologise: Learn to admit fault and apologise when you are wrong, and we can all be wrong at times. Do not add conditions to apologies or use the word "but" as this is not a real apology. Choosing to be honest, accept responsibility and apologise is incredibly powerful and good people will respect that and respond accordingly.

Acceptance: Hard work and positive thinking only get you so far, bad things will still happen, challenges will follow you your entire life. I take solace that life is not fair, for what is the alternative? That life is fair, and people deserve to suffer. No! Sometimes bad things happen to good, undeserving people, and we need to learn to accept that fact, carry that pain and move forward. We need to prepare ourselves to operate in the real world. Life after university will be unforgiving, without resilience you will not get far without breaking down.

Resilience exists in the natural world too, in Arizona USA, scientists have developed the 'biosphere 2' a 3-acre sealed site where they learn about our ecosystem by copying it in miniature. What they discovered, is that trees grown inside the sealed system would fall over before maturing. It was the exposure to wind and constant movement during their development that caused them to grow stronger and develop 'stress wood'. This hardship allows them to successfully mature without falling over.

Speaking as someone who was once the victim, it is not an easy task to change. It is an ongoing process to overcome this and sometimes you can slide back when there are feelings that something is unfair, but trust me, life is easier when you consider the positives, when you look to your responsibilities and have some stress wood to support you.

Difficulties come for each of us, from the most privileged wealthy person to the working classes, each individual find meaning in their own way, and it is this meaning that sustains us and drives us to be better and more successful.

Mental health.

When people speak of their university days, they often speak of the best time of their lives, an experience everyone should have and how they met friends that they still have twenty years later. However, that is not always the truth for everyone; 1 in 4 students report not having any friends in their first year, 1 in 5 report the same for years two and three. Increased loneliness and declining mental health are issues that have only gotten worse for the current student population.

The recent pandemic, or at least the government's decision in shutting down the population, has exacerbated this issue and this country will be feeling the impact of this decision for many years to come. A report from 2021 on university students' mental health has shown that during the lockdown more than half of students stated they felt lonely every day and many of these had avoided contact with others during this time. There is no doubt that enforced isolation contributed to mental health decline, with 40% of students reporting a deterioration since starting university and over half experienced many symptoms of poor mental health during this time.

What is more concerning is that 1 in 4 students reported suicidal feelings for the first time whilst at university, whilst nearly half of students from lower socio-economic groups reported the same.

Only a small number of students regarded the lockdown as the full reason behind their mental health decline, which suggests that even without the pandemic we would be facing a coming mental health crisis and the statistics seem to overwhelmingly support this suggestion.

Social media.

The 'monitoring the future' study released in 2017 shows that Gen-Z individuals (Born 1996 onwards) have less life experience than older generations. As a group they are less likely to drink, date or have a job. Instead, they spend more time on devices, phones, tablets, scrolling through social media.

The last 6-10 years has seen a massive increase in psychological disorders, specifically depression and anxiety, this pattern impacts females much more than males and often shows up in behaviour such as self-harm. On university campuses this effect is felt more keenly, with 1 in 3 students reporting some form of mental health problem.

This increased use of online apps and social media has amplified an already problematic issue. The prominent American neuroscientist Dr Andrew Huberman believes that many people are not successfully managing their relationship with pleasure because of social media. He describes it as pleasure without pursuit, there is no work involved, it is not earned.

This 'pleasure', whatever that may be, offers a dopamine hit, and like any drug, overindulging dulls the experience. When people become addicted, whether that be drugs, alcohol, or sex, you see a narrowing of the things that bring them pleasure. On the flip side, a healthy, positive life would be one that expands the things that bring you pleasure, your motivation, hard work and effort brings you the reward of pleasure, you can enjoy it more, knowing you have earned it.

We need to self-regulate our access to the things that brings us instant pleasure to maintain a balanced life. For many people who feel depressed it could be that they are over saturated with dopamine, they are addicted, and the feelings of depression are nothing more than the come down from their highs.

What is causing these dopamine hits? According to Dr Huberman, our habit around social media is carrying the lion's share of the blame. The best thing we can do is limit our interaction with social media, go phone free as much as possible and interact with the world the way we were meant to. We know that fresh air, exercise, and nature is good for our mental health, we know that if you are not connected to social media, the bullies cannot follow you home and we know that social media can become an addiction.

Dr Huberman also postulates that due to the way we process information in our sleep, our brain chemistry is changing even as we wake up. We should all avoid excess stimulus for the first hour each day when we awaken, use that time instead to shower/wash, make breakfast and dedicate it to self-care.

Too much mental stimulation, especially from social media can have terrible effects on our brain chemistry and cause imbalances that may echo the effects of depression. It should be noted however that this does not mean the individual is not depressed, clearly many are. Just that the overuse of social media and apps such as TikTok can echo the symptoms.

Despite the positive impact of messenger apps in keeping connected, on balance I believe social media is not a healthy addition to our culture.

Safetyism.

Safteyism is the obsession with removing emotional challenges or perceived 'threats' from people, challenges which were established in the previous chapter on resilience help young people to grow strong. This anti-resilience ideology is usually pursued on the basis that it is the good, decent, and moral thing to do, yet this can only be true if you are ignorant of the value of resilience.

This does not and cannot excuse bullying, harassment etc, but safetyism does not just stop at those issues, any ideas which can be emotionally upsetting however reasonable or necessary to discuss, become labelled threats to be removed from common discourse to protect people. And of course, bad faith actors when given this veto, will use it both as a weapon and to gain further victim status within a shared victim mentality.

In their book 'coddling of the American mind', authors Haidt and Lukianoff argue there are three modern 'untruths' widely held in higher education students, that greatly affect their psychological wellbeing. These untruths are:

Fragility: What does not kill you makes you weaker: A diametrically opposed viewpoint to the one postulated by Friedrich Nietzsche in Twilight of the idols. This overlaps with the principles of resilience which I will not repeat here, but Nietzsche's aphorism has been researched and proven by psychologists who suggest that previous trauma gives people the ability and strength to cope with future struggles.

Emotional reasoning: Always trust your feelings: Whilst emotions are ingrained in our being human, without context, experience, and wisdom they cannot be trusted for sound judgement. Anxiety and fear can also prevent you from making difficult decisions. The wisest course of action is to gather as much information as possible and making an informed decision. Not ignoring your emotions but not being ruled by them.

Us vs them: Life is a battle between good people and evil people: Any critical analysis of a situation will show life is rarely just black, or white. In a complex world anything political, ethical, or religious will have many shades of grey, there are usually third perspectives (or more) to contentious issues. It is entirely possible that the person you are in an argument with is wrong, but that does not automatically make you right, you could both be wrong. Unfortunately, we see this more and more with political activism. You are wrong therefore I am right. I am good therefore you are evil. It negates empathy and creates or exacerbates conflict which can increase the impact on your mental health.

Political activism whilst sometimes necessary or ethical carries with it a hefty price tag, it poses numerous mental health challenges, which to already delicate people trapped in a victim mentality and addicted to social media can have disastrous effects. Political action requires a lot of time, mental and physical energy which taxes an already difficult work life balance and can create emotional feedback to the wins and losses of your activism.

Whilst we all have issues we care about deeply; my advice is wait until you have established yourself before diving head long into the world of activism. Sure, if you care deeply about a topic, sign the petitions, join friends on walks and marches, after all being outside in the fresh air is good for you. But do not invest yourself too deeply at a time when you need to prioritize your studies and work life balance.

Self-discovery

Every individual is a unique being with great potential, self-discovery is a person's journey to discovering their true selves. The first thing to know is that we are not just the sum of our thoughts, we are not the ego and the doubts, the fears, and the ideas. These emotional responses and negative thoughts are unconscious defence mechanisms of our egos, our 'shadow self'.

When a person says something that you find offensive or triggering, is that really you being offended, or is it unconscious defence mechanisms from an unseen part of you? The only way to tell if the response is coming from you, or just your shadow self is to challenge your reactions. Are you offended because this person has crossed your core values, or is there an element of social expectation, groupthink, and ideology at the heart of that?

The idea of the 'shadow' was proposed by psychologist Carl Jung in the early 1900's, he believed the shadow was the uncivilised and primitive side of ourselves and that we need to fully see and accept our dark sides to be a fully integrated person. It is all about balance. When we can accept and face our anger we can set better boundaries, if we can accept and understand our sadness, we can feel more joy. Understanding your own emotions is important to empathising with others, creating better relationships, and resolving conflict.

When you can accept and control your negative emotions, you can start to focus on what brings you happiness, think of Maslow's hierarchy of needs, there are base needs that need to be met, security, food, sleep and so on. John Stuart Mill argues that to meet these needs may bring contentment, but real happiness comes from meeting your higher needs of esteem and self-actualisation. To help in understanding your shadow ask the following questions:

- Am I reacting from a place of love and care, or from fear and hate?
- Do I seek external validation, from my peers, from society, and from those whose ideas I profess to share?
- Do I use other people or addictions to fill a void I feel inside?
- Is the career I am pursuing my choice or the choice of my family and friends?
- If I lose my belongings, will I lose a sense of who I am?
- Does being alone make me uncomfortable?
- Do I care more about my group identity than my individual identity?

Engaging in self-reflection is a difficult but necessary skill to master to discover your real self. Thankfully, many higher education courses will include self-reflection elements. To become self-reflective, you must:

- Recognize your individual strengths and limitations.
- Be honest.
- Learn from your mistakes.
- Incorporate multiple perspectives and feedback into your own personal growth.

To reflect and grow, you must be able to admit fault, and accept criticism from others, even those with whom you disagree. It is a common failing for people to fall into echo chambers, which narrows viewpoints, ideas, and criticism. Allow yourself the ability to have your mind changed by good faith debate.

<u>Setting boundaries:</u>

I have spoken multiple times about the importance of setting boundaries in university accommodation, but it is true for all relationships. As part of your personal development and self-care you will need to determine what boundaries are appropriate and healthy for you.

Think of boundaries that exist in the world, a fence line for example shows what area is yours and what is the rest of the world, if people knowingly jump the fence, they are encroaching without permission into your space.

If you do not set boundaries, you allow yourself to be walked over. If you do not put up the fence, people will be taking short cuts through your garden and there will be no space for you, at its worst it allows bad faith people easier access into your house, your castle, where they can cause serious harm. Boundaries are drawn from your own core beliefs, opinions, and values. These are impacted by your life experiences and the society in which you live. Boundaries exist to protect your happiness and your needs, they are not rigid, as you change and grow, your boundaries will change too.

If the following statements sound familiar you may have boundary issues that need to be resolved:

- You have had difficult relationships, people will 'use' or control you.
- You find it difficult to make decisions.
- You try to please other people too much. This leads to fatigue and symptoms of mild depression.
- You regularly feel guilt and anxiety.
- You overshare private information.
- You do not feel others respect you.

It is not easy to establish boundaries, but it is never too late to start. It is ok to say no if someone asks of you something that will make you uncomfortable. Make room to put yourself first in occasion. Do not feel guilty about taking the last slice of pizza, especially if you have not had any yet. Do not put the higher needs of others ahead of the basic needs of yourself.

Self-care.

Self-care is not about indulgence, being selfish or greedy, its fundamentally about taking care of yourself, so you can be healthy and capable of carrying out work or your day and deal with the stressors that confront us. There are many elements to good self-care which can include:

Getting into a good sleep routine:
- Regular bedtimes and 'wake' times.
- Relax before bed, activities such as reading, or yoga are good for this.
- No screen time before bed or when you wake, use an alarm clock to reduce the temptation to scroll through social media in the morning.

Control your environment:
- Declutter and clean your room.
- Changing bedsheets regularly and cleaning your room can decrease the odds of you becoming ill.
- Spend time outdoors, get fresh air and take part in physical activities.

Doing things, you enjoy.
- Volunteer activities can benefit mental health.
- Watch your favourite TV shows.
- Play games or do something creative like drawing, playing an instrument.
- Socialising, catching up with friends and family.

- Plan 'me' time.

Ensure you have a healthy balanced diet:
- Cook with friends to increase the enjoyment.
- Plan meals to include a balance of carbs, protein, and vegetables.
- Avoid high salt and high sugar foods outside of a treat, drop the pot noodle and cook some pasta instead.
- Make sure you take vitamins and supplements if needed, vegans need B12 (found in fish, beef, milk, cheese, and eggs)

A healthy body can help cultivate a healthy mind, your diet and exercise should play a key role in self-care, and it is incredibly important to plan time for yourself and hobbies. Maybe consider it as a reward, "if I get this essay/section written today, tomorrow I will go to the cinema with friends".

Time management and organisation are so important to a balanced healthy life, writing a to-do list before bed so things do not cause worry and prevent you from sleeping. Having a calendar with due dates for assignments is a good idea, add in study time and 'me' time, allow for enjoyment, but do not allow that side of your life to take over to the detriment of your assignments. Balance is key.

Honesty:

I have mentioned honesty a few times when it comes to mental health and wellbeing. Honesty has both intrinsic and extrinsic value; I personally believe that all lies are immoral whether they be told with good or bad intents. Although a white lie told to prevent someone from being hurt is usually a compromise most people make (does my bum look big in this?), although care must be taken not to become accustomed to lying.

It is old wisdom that honesty is the best policy: Thomas Jefferson said: "Honesty is the first chapter in the book of wisdom". In the justice system, truth is the greatest virtue, in academia truth (Veritas) is a cornerstone of learning and excellence.

Without honesty people will not be able to rely on you and all strong relationships are founded on truth and clarity. Think about it this way, would you want someone in your life who was dishonest? So why be dishonest to others? People need to trust those closest to them and one lie can make someone doubt you, after all if you are lying about this, what else are you lying about?

Honesty speaks to your character and values; it shows respect, authenticity, consistency and often bravery and it makes you more reliable. Conversely it is stressful to maintain falsehoods, one lie leads to another, and it is hard to keep track of. The simplest way through life is to tell the truth.

The Science of honesty study from professors at the university of Notre Dame shows that telling the truth (lying less) can improve a person's mental and physical health over time. Honesty is important for people's wellbeing and self-discovery; without truth and self-reflection we are hiding from our own Jungian shadows. Shakespeare said, "to thine own self be true" and that you should not then be false to anyone else (paraphrased), meaning if you cannot be honest to yourself, you cannot be honest to others and cannot form meaningful trust-based relationships.

In the end we are only what others remember of us, are we dishonest and untrustworthy? seeking victim status? or do others see us as strong, honest individuals, overcoming adversity, seeking to be the best versions of ourselves. I like to think we can all be the latter.

About the Author.

Originally from Suffolk, Matthew Evans narrowly escaped a mundane career in security and now works in the action-packed student housing management for a university. An aspiring writer, self-defence enthusiast and tabletop wargamer. He has a wife, three children, Adam, Amelia, and Alice and currently lives in Norfolk

Printed in Great Britain
by Amazon

16633557R00108